Secret Dishes From Around the World 3

£25.00

First published in 2021 by Bounceback Books
Holyoake House
Hanover Street
Manchester
M60 0AS

info@bouncebackfood.co.uk
www.bouncebackfood.co.uk

ISBN: 978-1-9162650-6-6

Further information about how we source, research and adapt recipes for use in our community cookery school and fundraising products can be found via our website (www.bouncebackfood.co.uk) together with any updated credits.

Graphic design by Peter Lang.

Printed in Turkey. Production managed by Jellyfish Solutions.

All proceeds from the sale of this book will help fund future Bounceback Food CIC projects.

A CIP catalogue record of this book is available from the British Library.

Secret 3 Dishes
From Around the World

Acknowledgements

This book is dedicated to all of the members of our community cookery school. Without their support during another turbulent year, we wouldn't have been able to scale up our social impact and begin proactively fighting food poverty in new locations.

We also couldn't have completed *Secret Dishes From Around the World 3* without support from the 20 wonderful arts charities and social enterprises who were selected to represent the 20 cities where we are aiming to replicate our community cookery school model. They were instrumental to the success of our crowdfunding campaign and the artwork they've commissioned is absolutely superb!

Special mention must also go to the organisations and corporate partners who backed our crowdfunding campaign:

The Biscuit Factory Foundation

Thank you for generously supporting our 'Back the book' crowdfunding campaign and helping us hit our target ahead of schedule!

www.thebiscuitfactory.com

JMW Solicitors

Thank you for supporting our fight against food poverty in Manchester and helping turn our vision for this book into a reality!

JMW is a full-service law firm providing legal services and advice for both businesses and individuals. For more than 40 years, they have been fighting to achieve a positive outcome for their clients to get them the results they deserve.

www.jmw.co.uk

Partner Accountancy Ltd

Thank you for becoming our first corporate partner in Wakefield and helping to grow our social enterprise!

www.partneraccountancy.co.uk

Design Credits

Thanks to everyone on the Bounceback Food CIC team who has worked on the book:

Josh Rea

Josh is our multi-talented head chef who developed our secret dishes and also took the beautiful photographs that accompany each recipe!

He studied Photography at Manchester Metropolitan University and joined Bounceback Food CIC following our first social enterprise internship programme back in 2018.

Find out more at: www.bouncebackfood.co.uk/internships

Peter Lang

Peter is an experienced freelance graphic designer with over 10 years experience working in and around Greater Manchester. Once again he has helped us to create a stunning cookbook that combines art, photography and exciting recipes from around the world!

Discover more of his work at: www.peterdoesdesign.co.uk

Caitlin Buckingham

Caitlin is our highly skilled nationwide partnerships manager who coordinated the crowdfunding campaign that raised the funds required to complete this project!

She studied History and English Literature at the University of Birmingham and joined Bounceback Food CIC after completing our social enterprise internship programme in 2020.

Find out more at: www.bouncebackfood.co.uk/jobs

Funders

We would also like to thank our funders and supporters:

 ## The School for Social Entrepreneurs

Thank you for guiding the development of our organisation with your excellent Start Up, Trade Up and Scale Up Learning Programmes!

www.the-sse.org

 ## Social Enterprise UK

Thank you for continually promoting our social enterprise and raising the profile of our sector on a national scale.

www.socialenterprise.org.uk

 ## The Fore

Thank you for backing the expansion of our community cookery school model across the UK and helping us grow our central team in Manchester.

www.thefore.org

 ## UnLtd

Thank you for helping us to develop our organisation from a market stall in Salford to a nationwide community cookery school!

www.unltd.org.uk

 ## Our partner cookery workshop venues, foodbank collection points and distribution centres

Thank you for supporting our proactive fight against food poverty since day 1.

www.bouncebackfood.co.uk/charities

   The Art House

 the__GAP

Welcome!

Thank you for purchasing a copy of *Secret Dishes From Around the World 3* – our most ambitious fundraising cookbook yet!

In 2021 we began the process of transforming our community cookery school into an organisation capable of fighting food poverty nationwide. This involved mobilising volunteers, sharing resources and training groups of people in the 20 largest cities across the UK so that we could support our beneficiaries in multiple locations.

As part of this expansion, we wanted to complete the *Secret Dishes From Around the World* trilogy by partnering with a wonderful arts charity or social enterprise in each location (see pages 16-55) and commissioning them to produce an original piece of artwork for the country introduction sections.

It was fascinating to see how each organisation interpreted the brief. They either assigned the task to an artist they support from that country or created a research project for those involved. A description of how the artwork evolved accompanies each piece to provide additional context before 2 of our favourite secret recipes adapted for delivery by our central team in Manchester.

In another year where freedoms have been restricted we have once again shown that Covid-19 can't conquer creativity, collaboration and community spirit! We hope that you enjoy making our third collection of *Secret Dishes From Around the World*.

Happy cooking,

The Bounceback Team

Contents

Partner Arts Charities and Social Enterprises

Handy Tools & Alternatives

Recipes

Future Plans

Belfast

ArtsEkta

ArtsEkta is a multi-award winning cultural organisation that works to develop intercultural relationships at the heart of the community and is home to the Belfast Mela – the largest celebration of cultural diversity on the island of Ireland.

The brainchild of Indian-born Nisha Tandon, ArtsEkta was founded in 2006 on the principles of inclusivity, creativity and openness in all aspects of society. Ekta, a word of Indian origin, means 'uniting'.

Bringing together communities of Belfast and beyond, they create projects that inspire audiences to engage with the diversity, tastes, rhythms and sights that make up the multicultural life of Northern Ireland.

- www.artsekta.org.uk
- www.facebook.com/artsekta1
- @artsektani
- @artsekta

the___GAP

Birmingham

The GAP Arts Project

The GAP Arts Project is a youth arts organisation and cultural space based in Birmingham. They deliver multi-artform participatory projects that use creativity and culture as tools for young people to make sense of the world. Their public venue in Balsall Heath hosts exhibitions, performances, workshops, social events and more, supporting local community members of all ages and backgrounds to come together for conversation and cultural exchange. It is also where they run The MIX Community Café and associated food-related activities, including cookery courses run by and for young asylum seekers and free Iftah meal deliveries during the pandemic.

- www.thegapartsproject.co.uk
- f www.facebook.com/thegapartsproject
- @the____gap
- @the____gap

Bradford

Hive

Hive is a community arts charity based in Bradford that supports new and aspiring artists with a range of classes and access to specialist equipment including ceramics and woodwork. They also deliver arts, wellbeing and heritage projects within Bradford's diverse communities, using the city's rich textile history to improve the quality of life for residents.

➤ www.hivebradford.org.uk

f www.facebook.com/hivebradford

⦿ @hive_bradford

🐦 @hive_bradford

Hive

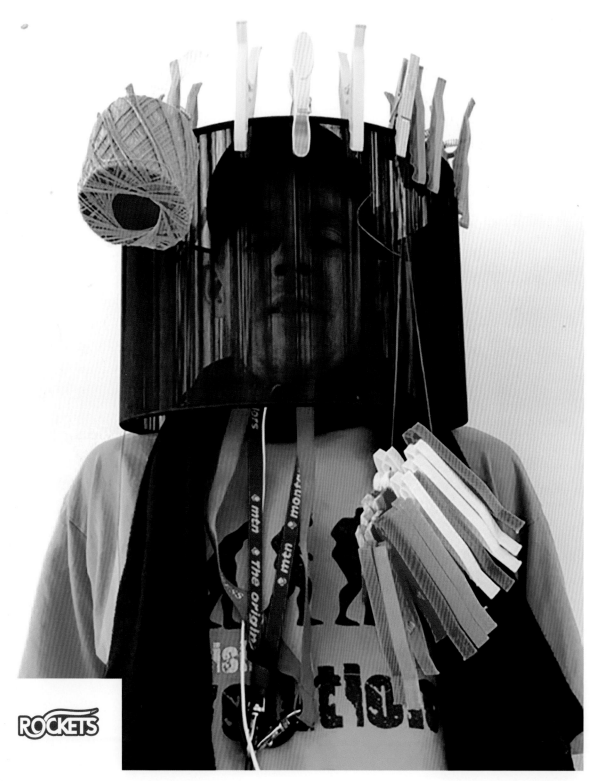

ROCKETS

Brighton

Rocket Artists

Rocket Artists are an inclusive group of visual and performance artists who challenge barriers around art, diversity, learning and communication. They offer artistic and professional development opportunities for artists with and without disabilities.

Their supported studios in central Brighton provide people with learning disabilities the opportunity to develop and learn new skills, be ambitious and creative with their own ideas and exhibit and sell their artwork.

Since forming in 2002, the non-profit organisation has been commissioned by the British Council, Tate Modern and National Gallery to deliver inclusive arts exhibitions, conferences and staff training. Their work, which celebrates diverse identities and art practices, spans the arts, education, NGOs and health sectors both locally and internationally.

▶ www.rocketartists.co.uk

f www.facebook.com/therocketartists

◉ @rocket_artists

𝕏 @rocket_artists

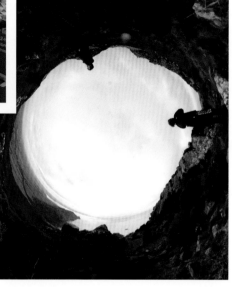

Bristol

BLACK* Artists On The Move

BLACK* Artists On The Move is a national arts development agency that supports black artists of all backgrounds and practices who are committed to excellence. They deliver a range of training programmes for artists focused on equality and decolonisation and run festivals and longer term initiatives in schools and community settings.

Travelling across the UK, their multidisciplinary team supports writers, theatres, dancers, musical artists, visual artists, digital artists, live artists and artists using craft traditions.

At their annual gathering, artists from all different backgrounds come together to immerse themselves in creativity and share current thinking, strategies and opportunities. It is also where they finalise their programme of work for the year ahead.

▸ www.blackartistsonthemove.com

f www.facebook.com/blkartmoves

▣ @blkartmoves

𝕏 @blkartmoves

BLACK

artists on the move

present

ECLECTIC

each event offers a creative

encounter

Cardiff

Women's Arts Association Wales

Women's Arts Association Wales (WAAW) was founded in order to offer women more opportunities to exhibit their work and as a protest against inequalities in the arts. WAAW support women across Wales interested in practising or exhibiting visual and creative arts in all disciplines. They also provide recreational activities designed to support and improve the lives of those who take part.

The organisation has charitable status and a large, growing membership. Their website and social media platforms provide details of upcoming exhibits and current issues in the sector.

➤ www.womensarts.co.uk

f www.facebook.com/womensartsassociation

📷 @waaw.2021

🐦 @womensarts

Coventry

Arty-Folks

Arty-Folks was founded in 1995 as a self-help group by people using mental health services and visual artists. Together they explore the potential of the visual arts to transform the lives of people who feel at a low point in life and are struggling with mental health challenges.

Over time a ground-breaking Art as Therapy programme developed that fuses art with self-development themes and, through the creative process, strengthens the identity and direction of people's lives and futures.

➤ www.arty-folks.org.uk

f www.facebook.com/artyfolks

◙ @artyfolks

🐦 @artyfolks

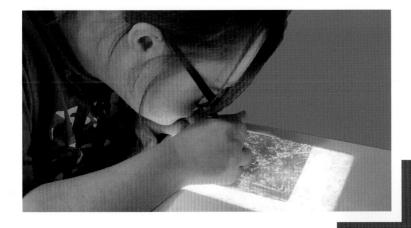

Edinburgh

Able Arts CIC

Able Arts CIC provides autistic people and people with learning disabilities experience in the creative industries. Artists get the opportunity to sell the art they create and receive 50% of the profit.

Founded in 2020, Able Arts initially provided discounted art workshops for people with additional support needs. Participating artists had the opportunity to sell their artwork. Throughout the pandemic, Able Arts changed their model and offered art competitions to local people. Artists with learning disabilities and autism participating in these contests have been able to sell their art, build their confidence and develop employability skills.

➤ www.ablearts.co.uk

📷 @ableartsedinburgh

Glasgow

Bazooka Arts

Bazooka Arts is a charity dedicated to improving health and wellbeing through participatory arts projects and arts therapies. They work with people of all ages and abilities in health, education and community settings, prioritising people most affected by inequality.

Bazooka's therapeutic arts specialists work with a wide range of artforms, including visual art, drama, dance, movement and film to support participants in making long-term improvements to health, wellbeing and quality of life.

➤ www.bazookaarts.co.uk

f www.facebook.com/bazookaarts

@bazookaarts

@bazookaarts

Hull

Absolutely Cultured

Absolutely Cultured is a cultural development organisation working to create opportunities and spaces for amazing cultural experiences to happen. Their ambition is to help make Hull an even better place to live, work, visit and learn – building on the success of the city's City of Culture status in 2017.

To achieve this goal they work in partnership across all sectors of the city, including arts, health, regeneration and education. Advancing cultural opportunities for the city, its residents and creative practitioners enhances Hull's cultural offer and increases the relevance and value of the arts in people's lives.

- www.absolutelycultured.co.uk
- f www.facebook.com/abscultured
- @abscultured
- @abscultured

Leeds

Pyramid

Pyramid is a Leeds-based arts collective and charity that help people with learning disabilities discover the arts, develop their talents and become world-class artists. They aim to disrupt the social and institutional barriers that prevent the people they support from being recognised, supported and celebrated.

They maximise their social impact with a combination of collaborative art groups, including a programme for people with profound and multiple learning disabilities, one-to-one creative support and professional development opportunities.

- ▸ www.pyramid.org.uk
- f www.facebook.com/pyramid.of.arts
- ◉ @pyramid_arts
- ◢ @pyramid_of_arts

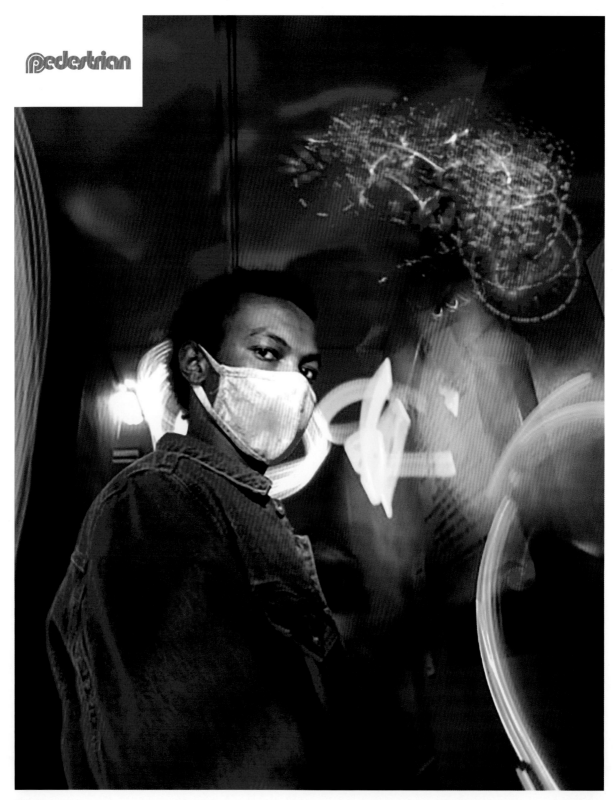

Leicester

Pedestrian

Pedestrian is an arts organisation that specialises in music and arts education. Since 1998, they have developed a reputation for delivering high quality creative activity involving education, training and outreach projects for young people, vulnerable adults and communities in Leicester, Leicestershire and across the Midlands.

Their participants are often socially excluded, not in education, employment or training (NEET) or experiencing disadvantage. Pedestrian believes that with the right levels of support and timely intervention anyone can achieve their goals - they call this 'Pioneering Potential'. They offer people the chance to explore their creativity through music, dance, photography, street art and many other artforms regardless of who they are and where they come from.

▶ www.pedestrian.info

f www.facebook.com/pedestrian1998

⊡ @pedestrian1998

🐦 @pedestrian1998

Liverpool

Homotopia

Homotopia is an arts and social justice organisation that produces, promotes and programmes the very best in LGBTQIA art locally, nationally and internationally. Every autumn they organise Homotopia Festival, the UK's longest running LGBTQIA arts and cultural festival, now in its 17th year. The festival offers an eclectic programme featuring theatre, film, dance, visual arts, family-friendly events, panel discussions and much more.

Year-round they also support emerging LGBTQIA artists from the Liverpool City Region through their ambitious QueerCore artist development programme.

➤ www.homotopia.net

f www.facebook.com/lgbt.festival.liverpool

⊡ @homotopiafest

𝕏 @homotopiafest

homotopia

41

London

ActionSpace

ActionSpace is London's leading and longest running visual arts organisation for artists with learning disabilities. They support more than 70 artists at their 3 dedicated studios in London and act as a development agency, advocating and promoting diversity within the contemporary visual arts sector.

By supporting artistic development and facilitating creative projects, exhibitions and events, ActionSpace have helped make a professional career in the arts accessible to artists with learning disabilities.

➤ www.actionspace.org

f www.facebook.com/actionspacelondon

📷 @actionspace

𝕏 @theactionspace

Manchester

Venture Arts

Venture Arts is an award-winning visual arts charity based in central Manchester that enables people with learning disabilities to reach their full potential through arts and culture. Exhibiting their artists' work regularly, in high profile galleries and exhibitions in the North West and nationally, furthers their vision of a world in which people with learning disabilities are empowered, celebrated, included and valued in the arts, culture and society.

Their studio provides a social, safe and inspiring environment from which their team of professional artist tutors nurture individual talents and creativity, supporting all participants to discover and develop their unique artistic identity.

➤ www.venturearts.org

f www.facebook.com/ventureartsmanchester

@venturearts_

@venturearts

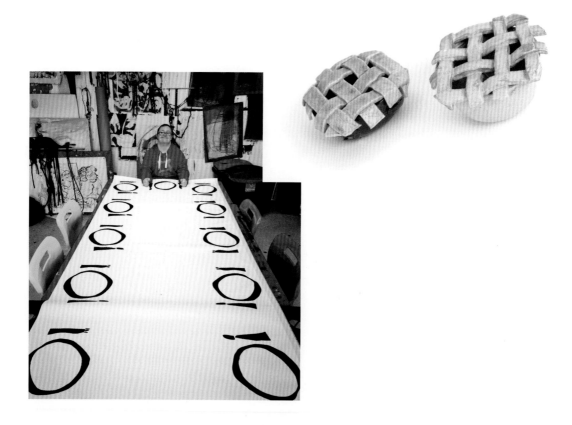

Newcastle

The Biscuit Factory Foundation

The Biscuit Factory Foundation is a charity which aims to nurture and develop the practice and appreciation of visual arts in the North East of England through an engaging and varied programme of creative opportunities.

The charity delivers a wide cultural programme that is accessible on a local, regional and national level. Their work includes leading on local cultural initiatives, such as the annual Ouseburn Open Studios event, engaging young people in artistic workshops, providing artist studios across numerous sites and commissioning local artists to provide public art.

➤ www.thebiscuitfactory.com/pages/the-biscuit-factory-foundation

f www.facebook.com/thebiscuitfactorynewcastle

@thebiscuitfactorygallery

Sheffield

ArtWorks South Yorkshire

ArtWorks South Yorkshire is a non-profit creative arts organisation that inspires and helps artists with learning disabilities, autism, or both to achieve their potential and develop important life skills through creative workshops and placements.

ArtWorks focuses on achievement, self-belief, collaborative practice and teamwork whilst supporting their artists to play an active role within the community. They aim to challenge people's perceptions of learning disabilities and autism by celebrating the creativity and ambition of their artists.

➤ www.artworks-sy.co.uk

f www.facebook.com/artworkssouthyorkshire

⬛ @artworks_sy

🐦 @artworkssy

Sunderland

Sunderland Family Arts Network

Sunderland Family Arts Network is a group of cultural and creative organisations in Sunderland, dedicated to bringing art and creativity to families. Set up in 2013 as part of the national Family Arts Campaign, the Network was created to provide arts opportunities to families in Sunderland.

The Network partners with a range of members including Creative Cohesion, Infinite Arts, Arts Centre Washington, Theatre Space North East, Northern Gallery for Contemporary Art, City Library and Arts Centre, Sunderland Museum and Winter Gardens and Creative Learning at Sunderland Empire.

They also work closely with More Than Grandparents, a charity that supports kinship families by providing a range of support services including one-to-one support, training opportunities and events that bring families together to enjoy new experiences and provide a little respite from their complex daily lives.

▸ www.familyarts.co.uk/networks/sunderland-family-arts-network

f www.facebook.com/fansunderland

Wakefield

The Art House

The Art House is a place for artists and audiences of all kinds to come together and engage with the creative process through a year-round programme of residencies, exhibitions, events, workshops and professional development opportunities.

Established in 1994 by a diverse group of artists, The Art House has become Wakefield's largest provider of studios and other artist facilities. The organisation's core mission is focused on equality of access and increasing diversity in contemporary visual arts practice. This is achieved by providing time, space and support for artists and creative businesses.

➤ www.the-arthouse.org.uk

f www.facebook.com/thearthouse.wakefield

📷 @thearthouseuk

🐦 @thearthouseuk

The Art House

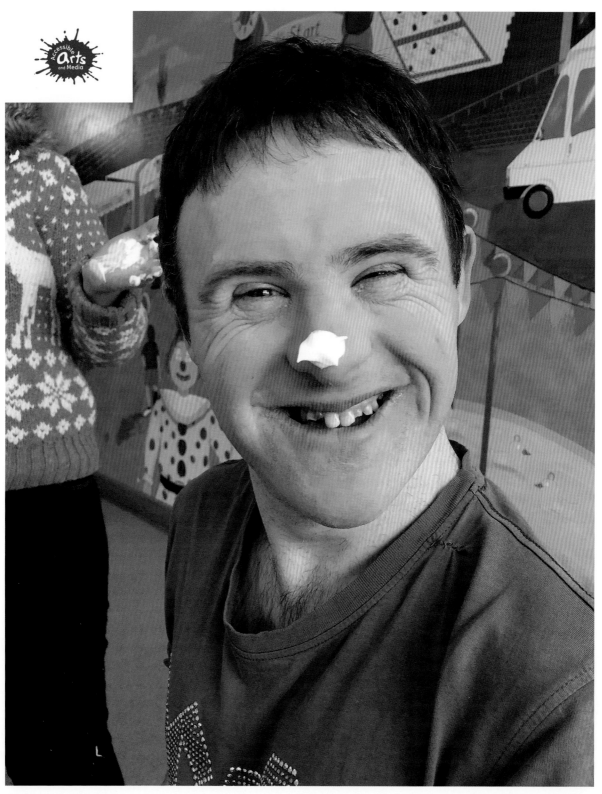

York

Accessible Arts & Media

Accessible Arts & Media (AAM) have been running inclusive arts and media learning projects in York since 1982. These include accessible music-making groups, singing and signing choirs, specialist therapeutic sensory activities and opportunities for young people and adults with learning disabilities to train as workshop leaders.

People who take part in their projects include disabled young people and adults, people living with dementia and people with mental ill-health. AAM helps them develop the confidence and skills to try new activities, make new friends and have more of a say in the things that matter to them. Everyone has lots of fun along the way!

▶ www.aamedia.org.uk

f www.facebook.com/aamedia.org.uk

◻ @accessibleartsyork

🐦 @aamedia_org_uk

Handy Tools & Alternatives

Here's our practical advice on a selection of kitchen utensils that can help improve your cooking!

Pans

A couple of medium sized saucepans and frying pans will see you through most dishes in this book. We recommend the non-stick variety as they are easier to clean, durable, require less cooking oil and are relatively inexpensive.

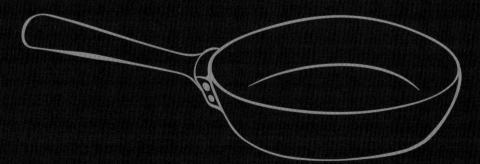

Knives

One well looked after and versatile knife will serve you better than a whole set of specialist blades. When choosing a knife, make sure you are comfortable with its weight and size. We recommend a medium to large chef's knife as an all-purpose home kitchen option. Small knives will struggle to chop tough vegetables, whereas a large and heavy knife can be tiring to use, especially if you are not used to using them.

Spice Mixers

For the strongest flavours, grinding fresh spices with a pestle and mortar is usually best. One made out of stone will work as well as more expensive options, such as granite. Once bought they will last a lifetime and they can really help bring your dishes to life! If you don't have a pestle and mortar, you can mix together pre-ground herbs in a bowl with a teaspoon instead.

Blenders

While the price of some premium blenders can reach astronomical heights, simple hand blenders can be found for about £10 in most larger supermarkets or appliance retailers. These handy little tools are great for liquifying soups, curries and purées. A half-decent one will also make quick work of awkward tasks like chopping nuts, though this can also be achieved by careful chopping with a knife. Blenders with a chamber fitting are also excellent for making Guasacaca (see page 145), Cocada (see page 146) and Gado Gado (see page 151).

Although blenders are perhaps not quite a kitchen essential, they are certainly worth considering especially if you find the labour of excessive chopping difficult or if you are cooking for someone who struggles with solid foods.

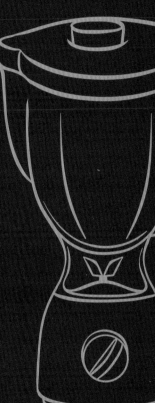

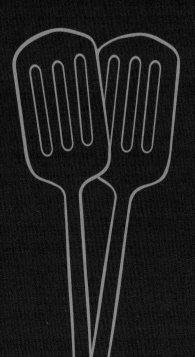

Spatula, Tongs and Spoons

When buying these kitchen essentials, you'll need to consider how frequently you'll use them and remember what they're best for! Spatulas are essential for pancake style flipping and are useful for scraping stuck food from the bottom of a pan. Tongs are good for flipping vegetables in the pan but not as good for trying sauces. Spoons are great for testing and stirring sauces but can make it difficult to flip food such as onion slices which can stick flat to the pan.

You'll also need to consider the material that utensils are made from. Metal and plastic tools are more hygienic and easier to clean. However, if a plastic tool is not heat resistant it can melt on a hot surface. Metal tools can damage the bottom of a pan when used incorrectly.

二〇十七年 正月 荣根

Chinese painting is one of the oldest artistic traditions in the world. Pieces that depict the landscape and creatures that inhabit it are often the main source of inspiration. Rong-Gen's contemporary Chinese painting, of a pair of ducks amidst a large lotus plant, on a lake near his hometown, reflects the traditional depiction of nature with a modern twist by using bold brush strokes in ink and watercolours. The lotus is a very important flower in the Buddhist community and in Chinese culture. It symbolises ultimate purity of the heart, mind and perfection.

Covid-19 stopped Rong-Gen from making his annual visit back to Shanghai, preventing him from attending his only son's wedding in October 2020. He has twice participated in ArtsEkta's yearly Mela event in Belfast's Botanic Gardens, demonstrating his amazing talent in Chinese painting to hundreds of visitors.

China

Title: Lotus
Artist: Rong-Gen Yin
Commissioned by: ArtsEkta

240g mushrooms of your choosing, left whole or chopped if larger in size

800g fresh egg noodles

1 onion (red or brown), sliced

1 thumb-sized piece of ginger, sliced

1 bell pepper, colour of your choosing, chopped

1 carrot, thinly sliced

2 spring onions, sliced

2 tbsps Chinese five spice

150ml dark soy sauce

100ml light soy sauce

6 tbsps hoisin sauce

2 tsps sesame seed oil

1 tbsp vegetable oil

1 ½ tbsps sesame seeds

1 tbsp dried chilli flakes (optional)

Chow Mein

20 Mins

Serves 4

Veg

The perfect dish for an easy midweek meal, Chow Mein can be adapted to fit whatever you have in the fridge.

Method

1 Combine the dark soy sauce, light soy sauce, hoisin sauce, Chinese five spice, sesame seed oil and chilli flakes in a mixing bowl then leave to one side.

2 Place a large pan or wok over a high heat and add the vegetable oil. Once hot, add the carrots and onion. Fry for 5 minutes or until softened, stirring throughout.

3 Add the mushrooms and ginger. Fry until the mushrooms are cooked through, stirring throughout.

4 Add the bell pepper. Cook for a further 5 minutes or until soft.

5 Next add the noodles. Mix in and cook for 2 minutes or until hot.

6 Add the sauce mixture. Combine and cook for 2 minutes, then top with the spring onions.

Chef's tips

Our version of Chow Mein uses mushrooms to make the dish suitable for vegetarians, but feel free to switch them with pork, chicken or prawns depending on your preferences.

Chow Mein

Saun La Fen

Soup and broth

2 tbsps rice vinegar

7 tbsps dark soy sauce

2 tbsps light soy sauce

2 tbsps sesame seed oil

2 tbsps chilli oil

3 tbsps Chinese five spice

2 litres chicken stock

200g rice noodles

Salt to taste

Base

6 garlic cloves, crushed

2 thumb-sized pieces of ginger, peeled and grated

1 ½ tsps Szechuan peppercorns

1 ½ tbsps sesame seeds

1 spring onion, finely chopped

5 tbsps vegetable oil

Garnishes

2 pak choi, chopped

120g peanuts

10g coriander leaves, picked

1 spring onion, sliced

Saun La Fen

60 Mins

Serves 4

A spicy noodle soup with a distinctive Szechuan flavour.

Method

1 Begin by making the broth. Place a large pan over a medium heat and add the chicken stock, Chinese five spice, sesame seed oil, dark soy sauce, light soy sauce, rice vinegar and a pinch of salt. Bring to the boil then reduce to a simmer, now leave to cook for 30 minutes.

2 Pre-heat the oven to 180°C. Roast the peanuts on a baking tray for approx. 7 minutes or until brittle. Leave them to one side when done to cool.

3 Now for the base. Dry fry the sesame seeds over a medium heat for 1 minute then place in a side bowl with the garlic, ginger and spring onion. Return to the pan and dry fry the Szechuan peppercorns for 1 minute then crush in a pestle and mortar. Add the crushed Szechuan peppercorns to the other ingredients and mix.

4 When your broth has cooked and your peanuts roasted, take a second large pan of equal size to your first and place the garlic and ginger mixture inside. Now take a separate frying pan and heat the 5 tablespoons of vegetable oil, when it begins to smoke carefully pour it over the base mixture. The combined ingredients will sizzle and give off an aromatic smell.

5 Turn on the hob and fry the combined ingredients for 30 seconds, then carefully pour your stock into the same pan. Add the chilli oil and mix together, reduce the heat to a light simmer.

6 Clean the now empty stock pan and fill with boiling water. Keep your frying pan to one side.

7 Add the noodles to the pan with boiling water and cook for 4 minutes. At the same time, fry the pak choi in the frying pan for 2 minutes.

8 Strain the noodles and portion into bowls. Use a ladle to cover each bowl of noodles with stock then top with pak choi, peanuts, spring onion and coriander leaves.

Chef's tips

Make sure you have 2 large saucepans plus a frying pan available before you start. To make this dish vegan, simply replace the chicken stock with vegetable stock.

Bayan Moradi is an Iranian Kurd living in Birmingham. The GAP Arts Project commissioned Bayan after exhibiting her artwork several times and as part of their commitment to supporting local young artists.

Bayan's digital illustration shows a scene of people gathering together and celebrating an important event. The inspiration came from her childhood memory of witnessing a wedding in a village where she was staying at the time. She remembers a big crowd of people passing in the street, many of whom were carrying food, gifts and sweets on their heads. A mirror was carried in front of the bride to bring light and happiness ahead of her new life. It was such a happy and joyful scene.

Iran

Title: Ceremony
Artist: Bayan Moradi
Commissioned by: The GAP Arts Project

Fesenjan

Fesenjan

105 Mins

Serves 4

250g walnuts

600g chicken, legs or thighs

2 brown onions, diced

4 garlic cloves, crushed

1 orange, peel of one half, zest of the other

400g tin of chickpeas, drained and rinsed

500ml chicken stock

4 tbsps pomegranate molasses

Handful of fresh parsley, finely chopped

½ pomegranate, seeds only

5 tsps ground cumin

2 tsps ground cinnamon

1 cinnamon stick

1 ½ tsps ground cloves

1 ½ tsps ground nutmeg

½ tsp ground turmeric

1 tsp black pepper

2 tbsps olive oil

1 tbsp butter

Salt to taste

1 chilli, finely chopped (optional)

A chicken stew with a unique sauce made from walnuts, pomegranate, orange and spices.

Method

1   Pre-heat the oven to 180°C. Once hot, place the walnuts on a baking tray and cook for approx. 10 minutes or until brittle and dry. Remove and blitz in a blender until a fine powder forms.

2   Place a large pan over a medium heat then add 1 tablespoon of olive oil and all of the butter. When the butter has melted, fry the chicken until golden brown on the outside but still raw inside. Carefully remove to a side bowl, ensuring any excess juices remain in the bowl to avoid cross contamination.

3   Add the remaining tablespoon of olive oil to the pan then fry the onions with a pinch of salt for 10 minutes or until soft.

4   Add the garlic and cook for a further 2 minutes.

5   Reduce to a low heat then add the ground cumin, cinnamon, nutmeg, turmeric, cloves, cinnamon stick, black pepper, orange zest and peel. Combine and cook for 2 minutes, stirring constantly to ensure the spices don't burn. Loosen with a dash of water if required.

6   Next add the stock, chicken and juices, pomegranate molasses, chickpeas and walnut powder. Mix together and bring to a simmer then reduce to a low heat. Cook for 45 minutes, stirring occasionally to ensure that the sauce does not stick.

7   Check that the chicken has cooked through, top with fresh parsley and pomegranate seeds then serve.

Chef's tips

This sauce is aromatic rather than spicy, so add a little chilli if you want to increase the heat.

400g basmati rice, washed

550ml water

1 carrot, peeled and julienned

150g plain pistachios, deshelled

70g almond flakes

1 shallot, sliced

Peel of half an orange, cut into thin strips

Juice and zest of ½ a lemon

5 tsps sugar

50g sultanas

70g dried cranberries, roughly chopped

6 dried apricots, roughly chopped

1 tsp cumin seeds

½ tsp fennel seeds

1 tsp allspice

1 tsp ground turmeric

4 cardamom pods, burst and shells discarded

2 tbsps vegetable oil

1 cinnamon stick

Salt to taste

Javaher Polow

80 Mins

Serves **4-6**

Vegan

Meaning 'jewelled rice', Javaher Polow has a mixture of sweet, bitter, nutty and spiced flavours typical of Iranian cooking.

Method

1 Dry-fry the almond flakes for 2 minutes or until lightly toasted. Remove from the heat and leave to cool. Repeat this process for the pistachios.

2 Add a dash of water and the sugar to the frying pan. Cook on a medium heat until the sugar dissolves and reduces to a syrup. Add the carrots, orange peel, shallots, lemon juice and zest. Cook for 10 minutes or until the carrots have softened to your liking, then remove to a side plate.

3 Place a large pan with a lid over a medium heat. Add the rice, cumin seeds, fennel seeds, allspice, ground turmeric, cardamom pods, cinnamon stick, a pinch of salt and 550ml of water. Bring to the boil then place a lid on the pan. Reduce to the lowest possible heat which maintains a simmer and cook for 20 minutes. Try not to stir or remove the lid. You can also add your dried fruit at this point however this is optional. Adding the fruit now will make it juicy and plump whereas leaving until the end will provide a textural topping.

4 Once the rice has cooked, top with the toasted almond flakes and pistachios, carrot mixture and dried fruit if it remains.

Chef's tips

Traditionally, barberries and saffron are used but we have replaced them with turmeric and cranberries as they are easier to source.

Javaher Polow

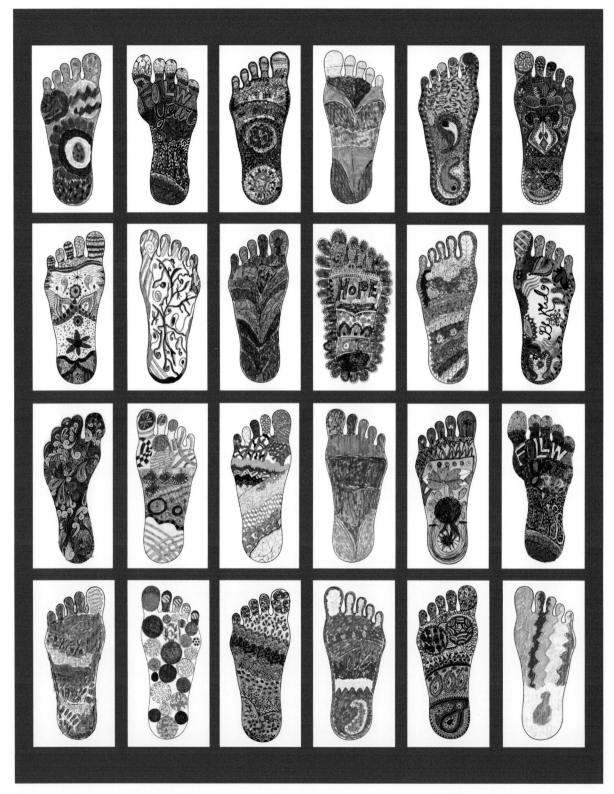

Hive work with many organisations across Bradford to deliver creative programmes. This collaborative piece was created by Hive's Flourish project participants at Roshni Ghar. The Flourish project encourages 'conversations through making' where participants engage with a creative activity and discuss any issues affecting their quality of life in a safe and supportive environment.

Roshni Ghar (House of Light) is a mental health charity that provides culturally appropriate, responsive services for South Asian women experiencing mental ill health. Umeed (Hope) is their support group for adult women with acute mental ill health. The group offers a relaxing, safe and creative environment that enables women to develop networks of friendship and explore self-help techniques.

Artists (from left to right): Aziz, Shamim, Tasleem, Tazim, Yasmin, Claire R, Claire, Parveen, Yasmin, Farra, Parveen, Zaba, Najma, Rabina, Ikraa, Shanaz, Zeenat, Zinat, Nusrat, Farra, Rozwana, Parveen, Lili and Perveen
Commissioned by: Hive

Bangladesh

Doi Murgi

For the marinade

6 chicken thighs

250ml Greek yoghurt

4 garlic cloves, crushed

1 tsp ground cumin

1 thumb-sized piece of ginger, peeled and grated

1 tbsp salt

For the curry

3 brown onions, diced

2 garlic cloves, crushed

1 thumb-sized piece of ginger, peeled and grated

4 cardamom pods, burst

1 tsp black peppercorns

1 green chilli, split lengthways

2 tsps ground cumin

1 tsp ground coriander

½ tsp ground turmeric

3 tsps garam masala

10 cloves

2 cinnamon sticks

2 dried chillies

Handful of coriander leaves, finely chopped

4 tbsps vegetable oil

200ml boiling water

2 bay leaves (optional)

1 ½ tsps brown sugar (optional)

Doi Murgi

80 Mins **+60** Mins
Marinating

Serves 4-6

An indulgent and simple curry that's cooked with an array of spices.

Method

1 Place the chicken thighs in a large mixing bowl then coat evenly with the remaining marinade ingredients. Cover the bowl with cling film and leave in the fridge for 1 hour. Remove from the fridge 15 minutes before you cook.

2 Place a large pan over a medium heat and add the vegetable oil. Once warm, add the cinnamon sticks, cardamom pods, cloves, black peppercorns, dried chillies, green chilli and bay leaves if using. Fry for 1 minute, being careful not to burn anything.

3 Add the onions and cook for 10 minutes or until soft. Add the garlic and ginger then cook for further 2 minutes.

4 Reduce to a low heat then add the ground turmeric, ground cumin, ground coriander, and garam masala. Combine and cook for 3 minutes, stirring constantly to ensure the spices don't burn. Loosen with a dash of water if required.

5 Return to a medium-high heat then add the meat and any leftover marinade. Stir frequently for 5 minutes then add 200ml of boiling water. Mix through and add extra water if needed, although the meat doesn't have to be totally submerged. Reduce to a simmer then place a lid on the pan. Cook for 1 hour or until the meat is soft and tender, stirring regularly.

6 Once the chicken has cooked, taste test the curry and add brown sugar to sweeten if necessary. Mix in the coriander leaves and serve.

Chef's tips

Use a full fat yoghurt for this recipe as this is what provides a thick glossy texture to the dish. Low fat yogurts will just turn to water in the pan. For a vegan friendly alternative, use plant-based yoghurt and substitute the chicken with approx. 700g of peeled potatoes cut into large chunks.

Dimer Chop

105 Mins **Serves 8** **Veg**

This street food is similar to a scotch egg, but with spiced potato instead of meat.

1½ kg potatoes, peeled and chopped into chunks

8 eggs, whole

2 eggs, beaten

150g plain flour

150g breadcrumbs

3 brown onions, diced

2 thumb-sized pieces of ginger, peeled and grated

6 garlic cloves, crushed

4 green chillies, diced

30g fresh coriander, finely chopped

1 tsp mustard seeds

1 tbsp cumin seeds

1½ tsps ground turmeric

2 tsps ground coriander

2 tsps garam masala

1½ tsps chilli powder

1½ litres vegetable oil

Salt to taste

Method

1 Boil the eggs for approx. 6 minutes then run under a cold tap, crack and peel then set to one side. At the same time, boil the potatoes in a separate pan with a pinch of salt for 20 minutes or until soft enough to squash with a fork.

2 Mash the potatoes in a mixing bowl then leave to one side.

3 Place a large pan over a medium heat and add 2 tablespoons of vegetable oil. Once hot, add the mustard seeds and fry until they begin to pop, then reduce the heat. Add the cumin seeds and fry for 1 minute.

4 Return to a medium heat then add the onions and fry for 5 minutes or until they soften. Add the green chillies, garlic and ginger then fry for a further 2 minutes.

5 Reduce to a low heat then add the ground turmeric, ground coriander, chilli powder and garam masala. Combine and cook for 5 minutes, stirring constantly to ensure the spices don't burn. Loosen with a dash of water if required.

6 Add the potato to the pan, mix until no white parts remain then add the fresh coriander. Remove from the heat then leave until cool enough to handle.

7 Cover each boiled eggs in potato mixture to create a ball shape. Lightly coat in flour, dip into beaten egg then cover entirely in breadcrumbs.

8 Place a large pan over a high heat and fill with the remaining vegetable oil. Once hot, submerge your Dimer Chop and deep fry until golden brown all over.

Chef's tips

Mango chutney and other dipping sauces make perfect accompaniments.

Dimer Chop

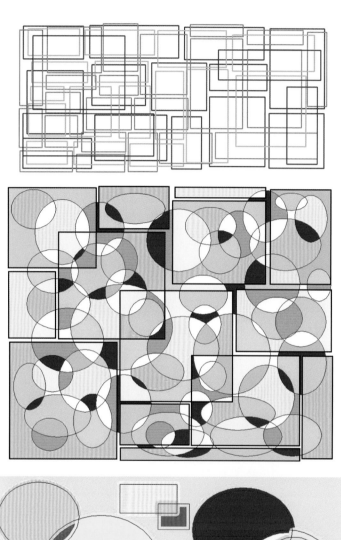

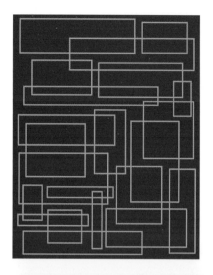

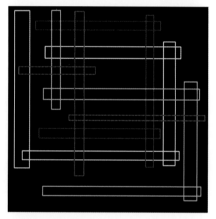

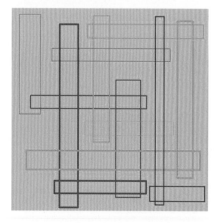

Richard Morris is inspired by graffiti and enjoys travelling to different cities and countries to find it. His artwork includes drawing, photography, filmed durational performance, installations, collage, street art and collaborative exchanges.

South Korea

Title: Drawpiles
Artist: Richard Morris
Commissioned by: Rocket Artists Studios

Bulgogi

Ingredients

550g beef steak, thinly sliced

6 tbsps soy sauce

1 ½ tbsps sesame oil

1 ½ tsps brown sugar

2 garlic cloves, crushed

2 spring onions, sliced

1 red chilli, sliced

1 thumb-sized piece of ginger, peeled and grated

1 pear, peeled and grated

1 tbsp sesame seeds

300g white rice, washed

400ml water

2 tbsps vegetable oil

Bulgogi

60 Mins

+12 Hours
Marinating

Serves 3-4

Marinated in soy sauce, sugar and fruit, thinly cut beef is left tender and packed with flavour before being fried and placed over a bed of rice.

Method

1. Combine the soy sauce, sugar and sesame oil in a large mixing bowl then stir until the sugar dissolves. Add the beef, chilli, grated pear, ginger, garlic and one spring onion then mix together ensuring that the beef is evenly coated. Cover with cling film then place in the fridge to marinate overnight.

2. Dry-fry the sesame seeds for 2 minutes or until a light browning appears. Remove from the heat and leave to cool.

3. Place a saucepan over a medium heat then add the water and rice. Bring to the boil then reduce to the lowest temperature, put the lid on and cook for 15 minutes.

4. Once done, place a large frying pan over a high heat and add the vegetable oil. Fry the marinated beef for 2 minutes or until crispy then flip and repeat.

5. Arrange your rice on a plate or bowl, add the beef then top with sesame seeds and the remaining spring onion.

Chef's tips

Korean Pear is used traditionally but normal pear, apple and pineapple are good substitutes. If you want to cut your beef extra thin, place it in the freezer for 20 minutes to firm up and then use a sharp knife to slice.

Oi Naengguk

40 Mins · Serves 3 · Vegan

1 cucumber, peeled and julienned

100g fresh cherry or plum tomatoes, quartered

2 spring onions, thinly sliced

8 ½ tbsps soy sauce

7 tbsps rice vinegar

1 tsp dried chilli flakes

1 tbsp sesame seeds

2 tsps sesame seed oil

2 tbsps salt

3 tsps sugar

500ml cold water

2 garlic cloves, crushed

5g dried seaweed (optional)

This cold soup makes an excellent accompaniment to hot, savoury dishes and is both refreshing and moreish.

Method

1 Dry-fry the sesame seeds for 2 minutes or until a light browning appears. Remove from the heat and leave to cool.

2 Combine the cucumber, spring onions and tomatoes in a large mixing bowl.

3 Add the soy sauce, rice vinegar, chilli flakes, sesame seed oil, salt, sugar, garlic and cold water to a large measuring jug. Mix thoroughly until the salt and sugar has dissolved then pour over the cucumber, spring onions and tomatoes.

4 Top with sesame seeds then place in the fridge for 20 minutes to cool.

Chef's tips

Keep the dish cool by adding ice cubes if serving with hot food. Dried seaweed makes an excellent topping too.

Oi Naengguk

Magdalena Julius Swallow lives in Mbeya, Tanzania. She was commissioned by BLACK* Artists On The Move as part of their commitment to support African-based and African diaspora artists. Magdalena was inspired by local traditions around food and used pencil drawing and watercolours to complete this piece.

Tanzania

Title: A woman cooks and smiles
Artist: Magdalena Julius Swallow
Commissioned by: BLACK* Artists On The Move

Mchuzi Wa Samaki

Ingredients

2 brown onions, diced

2 fillets of fish of your choice, cut into chunks

2 fillets of fish of your choice, whole, excess moisture wiped off, skin scored

400g tin of chopped tomatoes

4 tbsps tomato purée

400ml tin of coconut milk

3 garlic cloves, crushed

2 red chillies, sliced

1 thumb-sized piece of ginger, peeled and grated

4 tbsps vegetable oil

2 tsps coriander seeds

2 tsps cumin seeds

5 tsps garam masala

1 cinnamon stick

3 cardamom pods, burst

½ tsp ground turmeric

4 cloves

1 lime, quartered

Salt and pepper to taste

Mchuzi Wa Samaki

 90 Mins Serves **4**

This coconut based fish recipe is a great addition to the repertoire, especially for fans of dishes such as Goan fish curry.

Method

1 Place a large pan over a medium heat and add 2 tablespoons of vegetable oil. Once hot, add the cumin seeds, coriander seeds, cloves and cinnamon stick, then fry for 2 minutes or until toasted and aromatic.

2 Add the onions with a pinch of salt. Cook for 10 minutes or until softened, stirring throughout.

3 Next add the garlic, ginger and chillies. Cook for a further 2 minutes.

4 Reduce to a low heat then add the garam masala and turmeric. Combine and cook for 5 minutes, stirring constantly to ensure the spices don't burn. Loosen with a dash of water if required.

5 Add the chopped tomatoes and tomato purée then cook for 5 minutes on a medium heat.

6 Next add the cardamom pods and coconut milk, mixing as you go to ensure that no clumps remain. Cook for 20 minutes, stirring occasionally.

7 Add the chunks of fish and cook for 5 minutes.

8 Finish by cooking the fish fillets. Place a frying pan over a high heat and add the remaining 2 tablespoons of vegetable oil. Pat down the fish with kitchen roll to remove any excess liquid then place in the pan skin side down. If the fillets begin to curl up when they hit the pan, gently press with a spatula for 10 seconds then release. Cook for 5 minutes or until the skin is crisp, then flip and cook for 30 seconds on the other side. Combine the fish fillets with the sauce to complete the dish. Serve with lime quarters as a garnish.

Chef's tips

The pan-fried element of this dish is not traditional, but it really enhances the flavour of the fish. Alternatively, you can skip this step by adding the extra fish in at step 7 and cooking the fillets in the sauce. You can also experiment with other types of fish for different flavours!

300g basmati rice, washed

400ml tin of coconut milk

200ml water

2 tbsps desiccated coconut

Salt to taste

Handful of fresh coriander (optional)

Wali Wa Nasi

20 Mins | **Serves 4** | **Vegan**

Simple and fast, this coconut rice dish makes the perfect curry accompaniment.

Method

1 Combine the water, salt and coconut milk in a pan. Mix together to remove any large clumps of coconut fat.

2 Add the remaining ingredients then bring to the boil.

3 As soon as the liquid is boiling place a lid on the pan then reduce to the lowest heat possible which maintains a simmer. Cook for 15 minutes.

Chef's tips

The addition of desiccated coconut really amps up the flavour of this dish. You can also add a little coriander for an extra flourish!

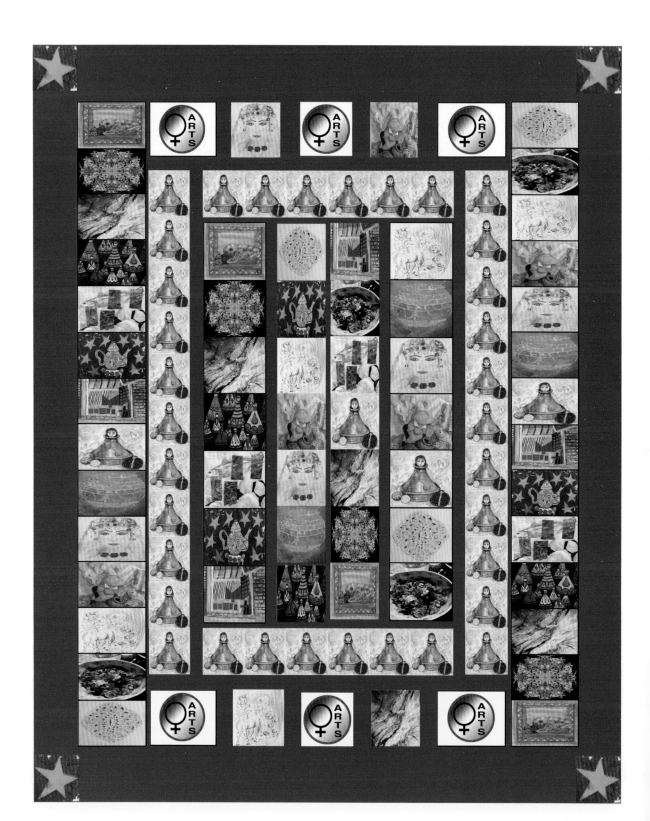

Women's Arts Association Wales were keen to support our fight against food poverty and nationwide expansion. They included details of the opportunity on their weekly bulletin and asked members to send in artwork inspired by Morocco. The pieces received were produced with varying media including digital print, drawing, watercolour, gouache, acrylic and stitch.

Their committee decided to use all 14 images submitted and asked the artists to combine the work in 1 collaborative piece. The design unanimously chosen lays out the work created in the style of a rug, incorporates the colours of the Moroccan flag and features all the artwork in an eye-catching pattern.

Title: Dreaming of Morocco
Artists: Claire Davies, Dianne Setch, Dilys Jackson, Helen Rowlands, Jacqueline Alkema, Jay Kynche, Jilly Hicks, Judy Stephens, Julie Shackson, Karin Mear, Patricia Clifford, Patricia Ziad, Sue Roberts and Sue Trusler
Commissioned by: Women's Arts Association Wales

Morocco

Fish Chermoula

For the marinade

Juice of 2 lemons

3 tsps ground cumin

4 tsps paprika

3 tsps ground coriander

6 tbsps olive oil

5 garlic cloves, crushed

45g fresh coriander, finely chopped

For the chermoula

600g white fish of your choice, bones and skin removed, cut into chunks

600g potatoes, chopped

200g plum tomatoes, chopped

2 brown onions, sliced

2 garlic cloves, crushed

10 olives

1 lemon, halved

500ml vegetable stock

2 tbsps tomato purée

1 tbsp olive oil

Salt and pepper to taste

Pinch of chilli flakes (optional)

Harissa paste (optional)

Fish Chermoula

120 Mins

Serves 4-5

With ingredients such as olives, lemon and coriander, this fish dish is both distinctive and delicious.

Method

1 Place the potatoes in a large pan and cover with boiling water. Add a pinch of salt and cook for 10 minutes or until soft. Strain and place to one side once done.

2 While you wait for the potatoes to cook, add all the marinade ingredients to a blender and blitz. Leave half to one side and use the other half to coat the fish in a mixing bowl. Cover with cling film and place in the fridge to marinate for 45 minutes.

3 Add the olive oil to a large pan over a medium heat. Place the two halves of lemon flat side down in the pan then fry until blacked and caramelised. Add the onions and sauté for 5 minutes or until soft.

4 Add the garlic and cook for 2 minutes. Pour in the other half of the marinade and cook for a further 5 minutes.

5 Stir in the tomatoes, tomato purée, olives, vegetable stock and a pinch of chilli flakes if using them. Mix together and simmer for 10 minutes, stirring occasionally.

6 Add the potatoes. Once hot, add the fish and cook for 5 minutes with the lid on or until the fish is cooked through.

Chef's tips

Traditionally, a preserved lemon is used but as these are hard to find our recipe uses a normal one. Harissa paste makes a welcome additional garnish. Serve with couscous.

Tagine

180 Mins

Serves **4-6**

An iconic Moroccan dish, tagines come in a range of styles and flavours.

Ingredients

1½ tbsps harissa paste

700g lamb meat, chopped

1 tbsp cayenne pepper

1 tbsp ground coriander

1 tbsp ground cumin

1 tbsp ground cinnamon

¼ tsp ground turmeric

1½ tbsps smoked paprika

3 garlic cloves, crushed

Zest of 1 lemon

1 tbsp honey

1 brown onion, sliced

1 stick of celery, sliced

2 carrots, sliced

1 green pepper, roughly chopped

400ml chicken stock

1 thumb-sized piece of ginger, peeled and grated

Handful of either dried dates, prunes, apricots or a mixture

Handful of olives

2 tbsps vegetable oil

Handful of almond flakes

Salt and pepper to taste

Handful of fresh parsley, finely chopped (optional)

Method

1 Dry-fry the almond flakes for 2 minutes or until a light browning appears. Remove from the heat and leave to cool.

2 Add 1 tablespoon of vegetable oil to the frying pan and raise to a high heat. Fry the lamb for 10 minutes or until brown and caramelised on the surface. To help this process, strain and save any excess juice in a bowl. Once done, remove all the meat to a side plate.

3 Return the pan you cooked the lamb in and fry the carrots, add the remaining tablespoon of vegetable oil if necessary. Cook on a high heat for 5 minutes or until caramelisation begins to appear.

4 Reduce to a medium heat then add the onions, celery and a pinch of salt. Cook for 10 minutes or until the onions are soft, stirring throughout.

5 Add the garlic and ginger. Cook for a further 2 minutes.

6 Reduce to a low heat then add the cayenne pepper, ground coriander, ground cumin, ground cinnamon, smoked paprika and ground turmeric. Combine and cook for 7 minutes, stirring constantly to ensure the spices don't burn. Loosen with a dash of water if required.

7 Add the green pepper, olives, dried fruit, harissa paste, lemon zest, honey, lamb meat and juices. Mix together then add the chicken stock.

8 Raise heat to a simmer, place the lid on top and cook on a low-medium heat for 2 hours or until the lamb is soft.

9 Top with the toasted almonds and fresh parsley.

Chef's tips

Tagine is usually cooked in a tagine pot, but you can get a similar effect in a large pan with a lid. Be patient when stewing the lamb and keep cooking until soft to get the best texture. For a vegan friendly version, use potatoes instead of lamb, vegetable stock rather than chicken stock and omit the honey.

Arty-Folks' Creative Peer Support Group that continued to meet throughout the pandemic felt honoured to be invited to contribute to this book and chose the tiny Caribbean country of Haiti for the vibrant art and folklore that reflects the country's African roots.

The group of 15 members first researched the rich history, culture and people of Haiti and learnt how they have suffered slavery, dictators, abject poverty and a devastating earthquake in 2010. They collected images on the internet to inspire their collages and mixed media artwork to tell the story of the spirit of its people and their determination to rise every time they are faced with adversity which is akin to the spirit of Coventry, their home town.

Each member created such powerful work and in the end it was incredibly difficult for anyone to decide which ones to choose for this book. Ultimately, they chose three images that worked well together and complemented each other for the final design.

Haiti

Artists: Arty-Folks Creative Peer Support Group

1 carrot, peeled and julienned

½ small red onion, sliced

270g cabbage, sliced

1 scotch bonnet chilli, sliced

7 coriander stalks with leaves, roughly chopped

1 tsp black peppercorns, whole

7 cloves

1 tsp coriander seeds

2 garlic cloves, sliced

400ml apple cider vinegar

2 tbsps salt

2 tbsps sugar

200ml water

Pikliz

10 Mins **+3 Hours** Pickling time | **Serves 6** | **Vegan**

Pickling is the perfect way to make the most of leftover vegetables. Give it a go with this simple recipe.

Method

1 Combine the water, vinegar, salt and sugar in a jug and mix until the salt and sugar have dissolved.

2 Arrange all the other ingredients in a sanitised pickling jar or airtight container.

3 Pour the vinegar solution into the jar/container filling to the top. Leave to stand for 1 hour.

4 Place in the fridge for 3-4 hours to pickle then serve.

Chef's tips

Try adding other spices such as fennel, cumin and star anise for a different flavour.

Griot

90 Mins · **+24 Hours** Marinating · **Serves 4-5**

This deep fried pork dish is delicious and traditionally served with Pikliz.

1 ½ kgs pork shoulder, cut into chunks

1 brown onion, sliced

1 shallot, sliced

2 spring onions, sliced

5 garlic cloves

2 scotch bonnet chillies, 1 sliced and 1 whole

1 green pepper, stalk and core removed, sliced

100ml fresh orange juice

3 chicken stock cubes

Juice of 2 limes

Handful of thyme leaves and stalks

1 tbsp cloves

Handful of parsley, chopped into thirds

500ml water

2 litres vegetable oil

Salt and pepper to taste

Method

1 Place the pork in a large pot then coat with lime juice and salt.

2 Add the onion, spring onion, garlic, shallots, scotch bonnets, green pepper, orange juice, thyme and parsley to the pot.

3 Break up the stock cubes and sprinkle on top, before using a spoon or your hands to mix everything together. Ensure that the stock cube powder and orange juice evenly covers the meat. Wash your hands thoroughly afterwards as raw scotch bonnets are extremely spicy.

4 Cover the pan with a lid then place in the fridge for at least 4 hours or ideally overnight.

5 Once marinated, place the pan over a medium heat and cook for 5 minutes.

6 Add 400-500ml of water (depending on how much is needed to cover your pork) then bring to a boil. Once hot, reduce to a simmer and cook for 45 minutes with the lid on or until the pork is soft and tender.

7 Remove from the heat and carefully strain the mixture with a sieve. Save the juices and leave to one side (see Chef's tips).

8 Pick out the pork meat and place on kitchen roll. Pat down to dry off the excess liquid.

9 Place a separate large pan over a high heat and add the vegetable oil. Deep fry the pork meat until reddish-brown and crisp on the outside. Place the fried pork in a bowl filled with kitchen roll, again to catch any excess oil. Be careful not to overfill the pan with vegetable oil and fry in multiple batches if necessary.

Chef's tips

Save the stock made from the cooking process to make a delicious spicy gravy.

Griot

Georgia Yuill is based near Edinburgh and has Down's Syndrome with learning difficulties. She loves all kinds of arts and crafts projects, creating pieces for everyone to admire.

Georgia really enjoyed researching Chile and decided to showcase the long, narrow shape of the country using striking colours associated with South America. She also drew a traditional pan flute, a Moai stone sculpture and the Chilean flag on top of a textured painted background.

Chile

Title: Chile is bacán
Artist: Georgia Yuill
Commissioned by: Able Arts CIC

4 frankfurters

4 hot dog buns or mini baguettes

1 red onion, finely diced

2 avocados, diced

100g fresh tomatoes, diced

Juice of 1 lime

Handful of fresh coriander, finely chopped

Mayonnaise to taste

Chilli sauce to taste

Salt and pepper to taste

Completos

25 Mins

Serves 4

A fun family meal with little fuss, Completos are a Chilean take on the classic hotdog.

Method

1   Begin by combining the avocado, lime juice, coriander, salt and pepper in a mixing bowl.

2   Pre-heat the oven to 120°C then place the bread buns inside to toast.

3   Add the frankfurters to a pan with boiling water and cook for 5 minutes.

4   Pre-heat a cast iron skillet or frying pan and raise to a high temperature. Remove the frankfurters from the water then place on the skillet and cook until scorched.

5   Remove the toasted bread buns from the oven. Cut down the middle and line with the avocado mixture.

6   Place the frankfurter in the bread bun and cover with red onion, tomatoes, chilli sauce and mayonnaise as desired.

Chef's tips

Substitute the frankfurters with veggie sausages and use plant-based mayonnaise to make the dish vegan friendly.

Pebre

Large handful of coriander, finely chopped

80g plum tomatoes, finely chopped

2 spring onions, finely chopped

¼ red onion, finely chopped

3 garlic cloves, crushed

6 tbsps chilli sauce

4 tbsps red wine vinegar

200ml water

1 tbsp olive oil

Salt and pepper to taste

Pebre

15 Mins

Serves 4-6

Vegan

This condiment is a delightful addition to many dishes and can be kept in the fridge or in a jar.

Method

1 Combine the coriander, tomatoes, garlic, spring onions and red onion together in a mixing bowl.

2 Mix the chilli sauce, olive oil, water, red wine vinegar, salt and pepper in a measuring jug, then leave to one side.

3 Pour the liquid into the bowl and mix thoroughly, ensuring all ingredients are coated. Leave in the fridge for a couple of hours to help bring the flavours together.

Chef's tips

Use less water and more tomatoes for a thicker texture.

The vibrant colours, patterns and motifs of traditional Ukrainian folk art provided a wonderful source of inspiration for the 12 artists and participants on Bazooka's Therapeutic Arts programme. They created this piece during the third national lockdown.

Together, through online workshops, they researched and designed each individual lino cut that contributes to this collaborative artwork which also includes a hint of traditional Scottish Paisley pattern. They are so proud of everyone involved as this was their first time doing lino cutting, guided via Zoom!

Title: The Sharing Table
Artists: Amanda Wallace, Heather Paton, Donna Frankland, Karen Calpin, Shamim Rashid, Ellie Brady, Bryony Murray, Gayle Robinson, Zoe Brook, Kirsty Robson, Tracy Gorman, Eva Harvey, Isla Thompson and Jennifer McCann
Commissioned by: Bazooka Arts

Ukraine

Borscht

 90 Mins **Serves 4** **Veg**

Sour and earthy, Borscht is a staple of Eastern European cuisine.

1.7 litres vegetable stock

400g beetroot, peeled, half grated and half chopped

1 carrot, peeled and diced

1 brown onion, sliced

1 celery stick, diced

4 garlic cloves, crushed

2 medium potatoes, peeled

70g cabbage, sliced

1 tbsp olive oil

4 tsps smoked paprika

5 tsps allspice

2 tbsps white wine vinegar

Handful of fresh dill, finely chopped

Handful of fresh parsley diced, finely chopped

Greek yoghurt to taste

Salt and pepper to taste

Method

1   Add the olive oil to a large pan over a medium heat. Once hot, begin to cook the onions, celery and carrot for 10 minutes or until the onions are soft.

2   Add the garlic and cook for a further 2 minutes.

3   Reduce to a low heat then add the smoked paprika and allspice. Combine and cook for 5 minutes, stirring constantly to ensure the spices don't burn. Loosen with a dash of water if required.

4   Add the grated and chopped beetroot together with the potatoes then cook for 2 minutes before gradually adding the vegetable stock.

5   Now add the cabbage and white wine vinegar. Mix and leave to simmer for 20 minutes or until both the potatoes and beetroot have cooked through.

6   Portion the Borscht into bowls then top with yoghurt, parsley and dill.

Chef's tips

Found in Middle Eastern food shops, strained yoghurt adds a great texture to the soup. However, normal Greek yoghurt also works well.

1 ½ tsps yeast

2 ½ tsps caster sugar

420g plain flour

200ml cold water

1 egg, beaten

2 ½ tbsps sunflower oil

1 tbsp salt

Handful of fresh parsley, finely chopped

6 garlic cloves, crushed

Pampushki

5 Hours   **Serves 6**   **Veg**

This tear and share loaf is a great alternative to a basic garlic bread.

Method

1 Add the yeast and sugar to a medium sized mixing bowl.

2 Place a small pan over a low heat and add the cold water. Raise the heat to body temperature then remove and pour into the mixing bowl. This may take less than a minute so be careful not to overheat. Test if the water is body temperature by dipping a finger in as it warms.

3 Mix the ingredients together then cover with cling film and leave to one side for 20 minutes.

4 Sieve the flour into a large mixing bowl together with the salt then mix together. Form a small well in the middle of the bowl then slowly add the yeast solution and sunflower oil. Mix as you go until a large dough ball forms. Use a dash of extra water if too dry, add a small amount of flour if too wet.

5 Keep the dough in the bowl and cover with cling film then leave to stand for approx. 30 minutes in a warm dry place.

6 The dough should now be malleable and slightly stretchy. Sprinkle a little flour onto a flat surface then knead for 2 minutes. Place the dough back in the bowl, cover with cling film again then return the bowl to the warm dry place. Leave for 2 hours, during which the dough will grow in size.

7 Coat the inside of an ovenproof container with a further teaspoon of sunflower oil. Carefully divide the dough into 8-10 small balls. Place the balls inside the container. Cover with cling film and leave for 45 minutes in a warm dry place.

8 Pre-heat the oven to 180°C.

9 Once 45 minutes has elapsed, remove the cling film and gently cover the top of the dough balls with a light glaze of beaten egg. Place in the oven for 15 minutes then remove and apply a second coat of egg. Cook for a further 15 minutes.

10 Top the dough balls with the garlic and parsley then cook for a further 2 minutes. Finish with a drizzle of sunflower oil and a pinch of salt.

Chef's tips

Be careful not to knock the air out of the dough as you glaze with beaten egg.

Pampushki

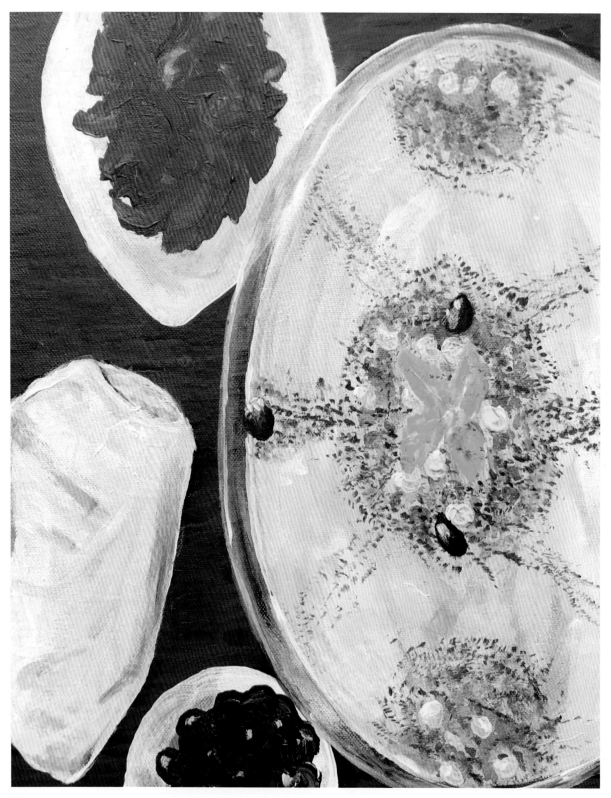

Born in Palestine in 1966, Amer Daoud has been a painter and sculptor for over 30 years. He is a defender of human rights and a graduate of the Beirut School of Fine Arts. Originally from Jerusalem, he has lived in Syria and Lebanon but he now lives in the south of France.

During more than 20 years of war, Amer never stopped painting. His work has been the subject of numerous publications, exhibitions and he has won several awards. Amer is also the subject of the BAFTA nominated film, *A Syrian Love Story* (2015).

Amer worked on this piece with photographer Sean McAllister who, after leaving school at 16, worked in a series of low-paid factory jobs in his hometown of Hull before finding a camera and filming his way into the National Film and Television School. Since then he has made BAFTA nominated films for the BBC, winning awards at leading festivals like The Sundance Film Festival and The Berlinale.

Sean's candid, frank films depict with extraordinary intimacy the lives of ordinary people who are struggling to survive and caught-up in a world of political turmoil and personal conflict.

Title: Fatteh and foul – my Syrian breakfast
Artists: Amer Daoud and Sean McAllister
Commissioned by: Absolutely Cultured

Fatteh

Ingredients

400g tin of chickpeas, drained and rinsed

300ml Greek yoghurt

60ml tahini

Juice of half a lemon

2 garlic cloves, crushed

1 tsp ground cumin

40g walnuts

4 pitta breads

Handful of fresh parsley, finely chopped

Handful of pomegranate seeds

1 tsp sumac

2 tbsps olive oil

Salt to taste

Fatteh

 45 Mins   **Serves 6**   **Veg**

Perfect as a shared starter, Fatteh takes the bread and dips format and gives it a freshness that is often lacking.

Method

1   Dry fry the walnuts in a frying pan over a medium heat, stirring regularly to prevent burning. Remove from the pan when brittle and toasted, then roughly chop and place to one side.

2   Place the chickpeas in a pan with boiling water and cook for 7 minutes. Strain in a colander when complete.

3   While you wait for the chickpeas to cook, combine the yoghurt, tahini, lemon juice, cumin, garlic and salt in a mixing bowl.

4   Toast your pitta bread then cut into slices.

5   Arrange the sliced pitta around the edge of a serving plate. Pour the yoghurt mixture over the cooked chickpeas in the centre of the plate. Top with the toasted walnuts, pomegranate seeds, parsley, sumac and olive oil.

Chef's tips

Adjust topping quantities to your own preference and try adding extras such as pistachios for variation.

100g fresh parsley, finely chopped

Handful of fresh mint, finely chopped

3 spring onions, thinly sliced

175g cherry tomatoes, chopped

100g bulgur wheat

300ml boiling water

6 tbsps olive oil

Juice of half a lemon

Salt and pepper to taste

Tabbouleh

 30 Mins

 Serves **4**

 Vegan

A glorious light salad for all occasions.

Method

1 Place the bulgur wheat in a pan with approx. 300ml of boiling water then cook over a medium heat for 15 minutes. Once cooked, strain and run under a tap until cold.

2 Combine all the other ingredients in a large mixing bowl. Add the cooked bulgur wheat, mix thoroughly then serve.

Chef's tips

Tabbouleh can easily be adapted to accommodate any other vegetables you have left over, just chop them up and add them in.

Tabbouleh

William Stapleton uses print and paint to create artwork and merchandise that celebrates Pyramid. He works in a development team with Carolyn Stiff and attends public events to help raise Pyramid's profile.

In 2018, William enjoyed the trip of a lifetime to Disneyland Paris where he was lucky enough to meet Mickey Mouse. Whilst soaking up the Parisian culture and indulging in its culinary wonders, he experienced the mouth-watering delights of traditional French pastries.

Inspired by his trip, William was compelled to include his new favourite pastries in his artwork alongside famous French masterpieces and notable architecture to highlight the country's cultural importance and rich history. He used a mixed media of oil paint and collage to complete the artwork.

France

Title: It's not just Disneyland
Artist: William Stapleton
Commissioned by: Pyramid

Clafoutis

70g plain flour

3 whole eggs and 1 egg yolk, beaten together

100g caster sugar

150ml milk

50g ground almonds

1 tbsp butter

200-300g raspberries and/or blueberries

Zest of 1 lemon

1 tbsp icing sugar

Salt to taste

Clafoutis

 45 Mins

 Serves 4-6

 Veg

A delicious, simple French dessert which looks superb.

Method

1 Pre-heat the oven 180°C.

2 Sieve the flour into a large mixing bowl. Add the ground almonds, 90g of caster sugar, a pinch of salt, milk and eggs. Whisk together to form a batter.

3 Cover the inside of a shallow oven proof cake dish with a thin layer of butter. Remember to coat the sides of the dish as well as the base.

4 Dust the base evenly with the remaining caster sugar, then arrange your fruit inside.

5 Sprinkle the lemon zest on top of the fruit, then pour in the batter. Place the dish in the oven and cook for 30 minutes or until golden brown around the edges.

6 Dust with icing sugar through a sieve, then serve.

Chef's tips

Traditionally made with cherries, here we have opted for raspberries and blueberries as they don't require pitting. The quantity of raspberries and blueberries you need will depend on the size of your oven dish.

For the salad

80g walnuts, whole

500g cherry tomatoes, whole

200g bacon lardons

½ shallot, sliced

5 garlic cloves, crushed

1 tbsp olive oil

30g fresh rocket

20g fresh basil leaves

50g spinach

70g Roquefort cheese, broken into small pieces

Salt and pepper to taste

For the dressing

2 tbsps olive oil

2 tbsps red wine vinegar

Salad Aveyronnaise

30 Mins

Serves 4-6

A warm salad that combines the richness of Roquefort cheese with walnuts and bacon.

Method

1   Pre-heat the oven to 160°C degrees.

2   Prepare two oven proof trays. One with the tomatoes, shallots, garlic, salt, pepper and olive oil mixed together, the other with just the dry walnuts. Put both trays in the oven.

3   Cook the tray with tomatoes for approx. 15 minutes or until they start to burst and the skins shrivel slightly. Cook the tray with walnuts for approx. 7 minutes or until they are brittle and toasted.

4   While you wait, combine the rocket, basil and spinach in a large mixing bowl.

5   Place a frying pan over a medium heat with a dash of olive oil. Fry the bacon for 5 minutes or until crispy and brown.

6   Mix the dressing ingredients in a pan then heat until boiling.

7   Remove the walnuts from the oven and roughly chop.

8   Pour the warm dressing over the salad leaves and mix thoroughly. Add the bacon, roasted tomatoes, shallots and garlic then mix thoroughly.

9   Arrange on a serving plate then top with the toasted walnuts and Roquefort cheese.

Chef's tips

Adjust the quantities of the dressing to your taste. Omit the bacon for a vegetarian version.

Salad Aveyronnaise

After an inspiring workshop with Pedestrian's Creative Art and Photography learners, Andrew Petrouis decided to create a piece that celebrates Leicester's twinned city status with Krefeld in Western Germany.

The artwork highlights leader of the suffragette movement in Leicester, Alice Hawkins. Alice stands surrounded by dress wear and patterns inspired by Krefeld's historic silk and velvet textile industry (it's also known as the 'Velvet and Silk City'). The composition selected also allowed him to illustrate the recipes in a more striking and distinctive manner, focusing not just on the final dishes, but the ingredients as well!

You can find more information about Alice Hawkins at: www.alicehawkinssuffragette.co.uk

For further details about the German Textile Museum in Krefeld, visit: www.deutschestextilmuseum.de

Germany

Title: The Lady of Leicester
Artist: Andrew Petrouis
Instagram: @andrewpetrouisart
Commissioned by: Pedestrian

Krautsalat

105 Mins **Serves 3-4** **Vegan**

This coleslaw omits mayonnaise and instead uses rapeseed oil and white wine vinegar for a fresher texture and flavour.

500g white cabbage, shredded

½ shallot, sliced

5 chives, finely chopped

2 tsps caraway seeds

3 tbsps rapeseed oil

2 ½ tbsps white wine vinegar

1 ½ tbsps salt

500ml water

Black pepper to taste

Method

1 Place a pan over a medium heat then add the water, caraway seeds and salt. Bring to the boil then reduce to a simmer for 5 minutes, mixing to make sure the salt dissolves.

2 Combine the cabbage and shallots in a heat proof bowl or container. Pour the water solution over the cabbage and shallots then leave for 1 hour, mixing occasionally to ensure you blanch the cabbage evenly.

3 Strain the water and briefly rinse the vegetables to remove any excess salt. Don't wash away your caraway seeds.

4 Add the rapeseed oil into a small bowl then incrementally mix in the vinegar, beating it with a spoon.

5 Pour the dressing over the salad and mix thoroughly.

6 Top with black pepper and chives, then serve.

Chef's tips

Fried bacon lardons make an excellent, non-vegan additional topping.

Krautsalat

Strammer Max

4 eggs

4 slices of bread

Butter

4-6 slices cured meat of your choosing

Sliced cheese

1 tbsp vegetable oil

Olive oil

Salt and pepper to taste

Optional toppings

Gherkins

Fresh tomatoes, chopped

Chilli flakes

Paprika

4 chives, finely chopped

Handful of fresh parsley

Handful of fresh basil leaves

Handful of fresh coriander

Mustard

Strammer Max

 10 Mins

 Serves **2**

An open sandwich that can be customised to your own taste, Strammer Max is a great brunch option.

Method

1   Place a frying pan over a medium heat and add the vegetable oil. Once hot, begin to fry your eggs.

2   While you wait for the eggs to cook, toast your bread either in a toaster or under the grill.

3   Butter your toast then arrange your cured meat and slices of cheese on top.

4   Once cooked, place your eggs on top of the cured meat and slices of cheese.

5   Drizzle with olive oil then season with salt and pepper. Add the optional toppings to your preference.

Chef's tips

Mix and match between the toppings listed and see which combination works best for you.

Christian Asare is a Black British multidisciplinary artist of Ghanaian heritage based in Manchester. A trained choreographer and contemporary dancer with a specialisation in Afro contemporary dance, he is also an independent fine artist, painting in oils with a focus on uplifting Afrocentric imagery, Afrofuturism, portraiture and abstraction.

Christian's artwork features the Sankofa symbol, one of the many traditional Adinkra symbols intrinsic to Ghanaian culture. The Sankofa forms part of a traditional carved stool which is holding a plate of Kelewele, a fried plantain dish. Christian painted the sky in red and gold which, together with the green in the trees, represent the colours in the Ghanaian flag.

Ghana

Title: Sankofa
Artist: Christian Asare
Commissioned by: Homotopia

Kelewele

Ingredients

3 yellow plantains, peel removed, cut into chunks

1 ½ litres vegetable oil

3 tbsps cayenne pepper

½ tbsp ginger powder

1 tbsp garlic granules

2 tbsps salt

1 brown onion, roughly chopped

1 tsp ground cloves

1 tsp black pepper

1 tbsp ground cinnamon

1 tsp ground nutmeg

3 garlic cloves, crushed

1 thumb-sized piece of ginger, peeled and grated

5 cardamom pods, burst and shells discarded

30g peanuts

Handful of fresh coriander leaves (optional)

Kelewele

 60 Mins

 Serves **4**

 Vegan

Deep fried in a mix of spices, this plantain recipe is an excellent side dish to share.

Method

1 Pre-heat the oven to 180°C. Roast the peanuts on a baking tray for approx. 7 minutes or until they are brown, then leave to one side to cool.

2 Add the cayenne pepper, fresh ginger, crushed garlic cloves, salt, black pepper, cardamom, garlic granules, ginger powder, onion, cinnamon and nutmeg to a blender then blitz until the mixture has an even consistency.

3 Place the plantain chunks in a large mixing bowl and coat with the blended mixture, then leave to one side for 20 minutes.

4 Fill a large pan with the vegetable oil then raise to a high heat. Once hot, carefully add the plantain chunks and cook for 5 minutes or until the plantain is soft and brown on the outside. Cook in batches if this is more manageable and be wary of the oil spitting.

5 Once cooked, add the plantain to a bowl filled with kitchen roll and leave for 30 seconds to allow any excess oil to be absorbed. Transfer the cooked chunks of plantain to a serving plate then top with peanuts and coriander.

Chef's tips

Try not to stir the plantain while it cooks as the spice mix will drop off.

Chicken stew

1kg chicken thighs

1 scotch bonnet chilli, whole

40ml water

125g fresh tomatoes

2 tbsps tomato purée

2 bay leaves

1 tbsp salt

1 red onion, roughly chopped

2 thumb-sized pieces of ginger, peeled and roughly chopped

1 green chilli, roughly chopped

5 garlic cloves, roughly chopped

1 ½ tbsps fresh thyme leaves

1 tsp black pepper

1 tbsp fennel seeds

½ tbsp cumin seeds

1 tsp cloves

3 tbsps vegetable oil

Broth

1 red onion, quartered

250g fresh tomatoes, whole

1 red bell pepper, roughly chopped into large pieces

1 aubergine, cut into large chunks

800ml chicken stock

8 okra, whole

Handful of fresh basil leaves, whole

1.2 litres boiling water

150ml of water (optional)

Light Soup

105 Mins

Serves **4-6**

A memorable West African stew rich with chicken juice, okra, aubergine and spices.

Method

1 Begin with the chicken stew by combining 40ml water, 125g of fresh tomatoes, 1 red onion, ginger, green chilli, garlic, thyme leaves, black pepper, fennel seeds, cumin seeds, salt and cloves in a blender then blitz.

2 Place a large pan over a medium heat and add the vegetable oil. Once hot, add the chicken thighs, scotch bonnet, bay leaves, tomato purée and blended ingredients from step 1. Mix together so that the meat is evenly coated. Cook for 30 minutes with the lid on, stirring and turning the meat regularly.

3 While you wait for the chicken to cook, prepare the broth by placing a second large pan over a medium heat on a separate hob with 1.2 litres of boiling water. Add the quartered red onion, 250g of fresh tomatoes, red bell pepper and half of the aubergine chunks. Boil for 10 minutes or until the onion and aubergine are soft. Once cooked, strain the vegetables and blend. Press the blended mixture through a sieve into a bowl. Save the juice and discard the pulp, get as much liquid as possible.

4 Prepare the chicken stock. Combine with the vegetable juice from the previous step then carefully pour the mixture into the pan with the chicken and mix together. Raise the heat to a simmer then cook with the lid on for 15 minutes, stirring occasionally.

5 Add the remaining aubergine and okra to the dish then cook for 20 minutes or until both vegetables are soft.

6 Test the spice level of the dish and add additional water if it is too hot. Finish by adding the fresh basil leaves.

Chef's tips

This dish can be made with a range of different protein, including fish and lamb. If using lamb, follow the cooking instructions for chicken but cook until the meat begins to fall apart. This may take longer depending on the cut, so be patient. If using fish, cut into large chunks and add to the pan at step 5. Fufu is traditionally served with light soup but bread or dumplings also work well.

Light Soup

Thomas Owen was inspired by images of Croatian culture, folk costumes and the national flag. The red check pattern of the Croatian flag and the national team's football shirt, uniforms of the National Guard and traditional embroidery patterns are all represented in his illustration. Thomas pulled all these references together to capture the essence of Croatia and interpreted them in his own vibrant drawing style.

Croatia

Title: Croatia
Artist: Thomas Owen
Commissioned by: ActionSpace

Brudet

60 Mins

Serves **4**

A seafood dish with a tomato base, Brudet can be adapted to whichever fish and shellfish you have available.

1 white onion, sliced

10 garlic cloves, crushed

1 red chilli, split in half

30g fresh parsley, finely chopped

2 lemons, 1 juiced and 1 quartered

300g mussels or prawns

700g fish of your choosing, cut into large chunks

2 400g tins of tomatoes

2 tbsps tomato purée

2 tbsps olive oil

300ml fish stock

2 tbsps butter

Salt and pepper to taste

Method

1 Check to ensure that each mussel is still alive by taking any that have opened and firmly tapping them on a chopping board – if they then don't close, discard immediately.

2 Debeard the mussels by sharply pulling the hair-like filament towards the hinge of the mussel until removed.

3 Thoroughly clean the remaining alive mussels (all closed) by using the back of a butter knife or scrubbing brush to scrape away any barnacles. You can also briefly rinse the mussels under running water to remove any remaining dirt however don't submerge them as this will kill the mussels.

4 Place in a bowl and cover with a damp cloth. Leave in the fridge until required in step 10.

5 Place a large pan over a medium heat and add the olive oil. Once hot, add the onion and fry until soft. Then add the garlic and chilli. Cook for 2 minutes.

6 Next add the tinned tomatoes and tomato purée. Cook for 5 minutes mixing as you go.

7 Add the fish stock and half of the parsley. Mix and allow to simmer for 10 minutes.

8 With the sauce simmering, add the chunks of fish and cook for a further 5 minutes.

9 Add the butter. As it melts, use a spoon to spread to different parts of the pan.

10 Rest the mussels on top of the sauce and cook with the lid on for approx. 5-7 minutes or until the shells have fully opened. The mussels should have solidified and come away from the shells.

11 Top with the remaining parsley and lemon juice, then serve with quartered lemon pieces.

Chef's tips

If you decide to use prawns instead of mussels, add these in at step 10 but ensure they are submerged before placing a lid on the pan. Cook until pink – this may take up to 7 minutes depending on the size of your prawns and how much room you have in the pan.

450g bread flour

1 tsp yeast

1 tbsp sugar

120ml milk

240ml water

1 tsp salt

Lepinja

4 Hours

Serves 6

Veg

A triple prove process ensures that this bread has a soft, tearable texture that is great for mopping up juices and soups.

Method

1 Place a medium pan over a low heat and add the milk, warming to body temperature. Check by dipping your finger in, don't let the milk become too hot. Remove the milk to a bowl then mix in the sugar and yeast. Leave to react for 10 minutes.

2 Add the water to the milk and mix together.

3 Sieve the bread flour and salt into a large mixing bowl. Slowly add the milk solution, stirring gradually until a wet dough forms.

4 Sprinkle a little extra flour onto a flat surface and your hands, then begin to knead the dough by hand for at least 10 minutes. Once done, return to the mixing bowl and cover with cling film to prove for 1 hour.

5 After 1 hour, remove the dough from the bowl and repeat step 4 for the second prove.

6 Prepare a baking tray with greaseproof paper then leave to one side. Return to the floured surface and divide your dough into 6 equally sized balls. Knead each for 2 minutes then use a rolling pin to flatten each into roughly circular discs approx. 2 cm in thickness.

7 Carefully tuck the outer edges of the discs underneath until a dome-like bun shape has formed, which is fully supported in the middle. Place on the baking tray and cover with cling film for a final 20 minute prove.

8 Pre-heat the oven to its highest possible temperature. Place a separate baking tray filled with water at the bottom of the oven. This will provide steam to ensure a nice crust on the buns.

9 Remove the cling film and bake the breads for 10 minutes or until a golden-brown crust has formed.

Chef's tips

Use oat milk if you don't consume dairy. Don't forget to put the tray of water in the oven!

Croatia

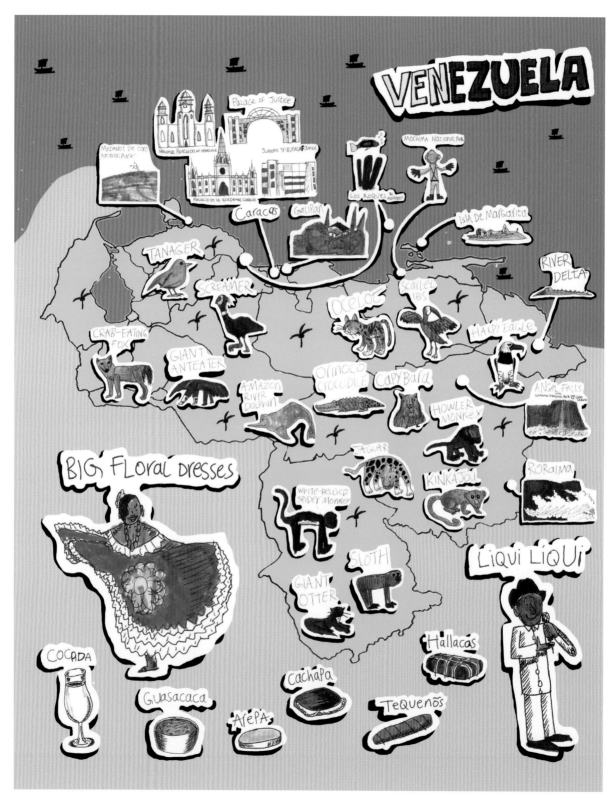

As part of his research, Justin P Lees discovered that Venezuela is famous for interesting wild animals, amazing landscapes, different foods, traditional clothes and that Caracas is the capital city. Justin drew a map of the shape of the country then decided to include everything he researched in his illustration.

James from Venture Arts helped Justin research illustrated maps and they discussed the best way to make them and which design software to use. Firstly, Justin drew pictures on small square paper using fine liner and felt tip pens, then they scanned them in. They used Procreate on an iPad to cut them out digitally. Finally, Justin arranged them all in the right places on the map to create his final illustration.

Title: Venezuela
Artist: Justin P Lees
Website: www.justinplees.com
Commissioned by: Venture Arts

Venezuela

Guasacaca

2 avocados, diced

30g fresh coriander,
chopped

30g fresh parsley,
chopped

5 garlic cloves, crushed

½ red onion, diced

1 green bell pepper,
core and stalk removed,
chopped

Juice of 2 limes

2 green chillies, chopped

2 ½ tbsps olive oil

Salt and pepper to taste

Guasacaca

 15 Mins **Serves 6** **Vegan**

A versatile condiment that can tie together a range of dishes.

Method

1   Place all the ingredients in a blender and blitz!

Chef's tips

If you want a more sauce-like texture, add more olive oil and lime juice. For a thicker texture akin to guacamole, use less olive oil.

400g desiccated coconut

600ml milk or coconut water

2 ½ tsps salt

9 tbsps condensed milk

5 tbsps vanilla extract

8 ice cubes

Ground cinnamon, for dusting

Cocada

20 Mins

Serves 2

Veg

A sweet drink that is perfect for a summer's day.

Method

1 Place the desiccated coconut in a bowl and cover with boiling water. Leave for 5 minutes then drain with a sieve and run under a cold tap until all the heat has left the coconut.

2 Combine all remaining ingredients, apart from the ground cinnamon, in a blender and blitz.

3 Strain the liquid into 2 drinking glasses using a sieve.

4 Use a tablespoon to add as much of the remaining pulp back into the drink to your preference then dust with ground cinnamon.

Chef's tips

Fresh coconut is traditionally used, but desiccated coconut is less labour intensive and available all year round. Adjust the texture to your liking by adding more or less of the pulp back into the mixture. For a vegan friendly alternative, use coconut water and a plant-based condensed milk.

Cocada

As a multimedia artist, Breezy Willows has always been fascinated by the designs and motifs found in East Asian artwork, specifically in woodblock prints and Irezumi tattoos.

The subject for this piece was drawn from the study of Balinese masks used in traditional dance, theatre and worship. The Garuda is the national symbol of Indonesia, representing creative energy, independence and greatness.

Breezy hoped to depict Indonesia's colourful roots whilst recognising its rapid expansion as a newly industrialised country, determining the best medium to achieve this was digital painting. He was commissioned to produce this piece by The Biscuit Factory Foundation, a charity based in Newcastle upon Tyne that provides creative opportunities to artists, all over the North East.

Indonesia

Artist: Breezy Willows
Commissioned by: The Biscuit Factory Foundation

Gado Gado

45 Mins

Serves 2-4

Perfect as a shared starter or side dish, this salad includes a delicious peanut dipping sauce.

Method

1 Bring a large pan of water to the boil and add the 2 eggs. Cook for approx. 7 minutes then run under a cold tap until cool. Crack, peel and halve the eggs then set to one side.

2 Add the potatoes to the boiling water and cook for 10 minutes or until a fork can easily pierce them.

3 Combine all sauce ingredients together in a blender and blitz. Spread the sauce around half of each serving bowl.

4 Once the potatoes have cooked, strain and run them under the cold tap to cool.

5 Arrange all ingredients in the serving bowls and top with sesame seed oil.

Chef's tips

Top with mint and coriander leaves for a little extra colour and toasted sesame seeds for texture. Tofu and prawn crackers are also traditionally used. If kecap manis cannot be found, add extra soy sauce. Omit the fish sauce and eggs to make the dish vegan.

For the paste

50g ginger, peeled and roughly chopped

5 garlic cloves, roughly chopped

3 shallots, roughly chopped

15g cashew nuts

8-12 mild dried chillies, roughly chopped and rehydrated with boiling water

40g dried shrimp, rehydrated with boiling water

3 tbsps fish sauce

½ tsp ground turmeric

2 tsps coriander seeds

1 tsp cayenne pepper

2 lemongrass stems, chopped

3 tsps shrimp paste (optional)

For the soup

Handful of fresh coriander, stems and leaves intact

Handful of fresh mint, stems and leaves intact

1 litre fish stock

800ml of coconut milk

2 lemongrass stems, split lengthways

3 tbsps brown sugar

2 tbsps vegetable oil

12 large prawns

225g rice noodles

Optional toppings

Handful of cashew nuts

Handful of coriander leaves

3 spring onions, roughly chopped

340g fried tofu

Laksa

90 Mins

Serves 4

A spicy seafood curry with an incredibly fresh flavour.

Method

1 Combine all the paste ingredients in a blender, aside from any excess water from the rehydrated chillies and shrimp, then blitz.

2 Place a large pan over a medium heat and add 1 tablespoon of vegetable oil. Once hot, reduce to a low heat then add the paste. Fry for 30 minutes, stirring continuously, until the paste has a deep reddish-brown colour. Loosen the paste with a dash of water from time to time if the paste starts to stick to the bottom of the pan.

3 Next add the fish stock and mix through so that there are no clumps of paste. Raise the heat to a simmer and add the lemongrass. Partially cover with a lid and cook down for 10 minutes.

4 Slowly add the coconut milk and mix until an even consistency forms. Add the brown sugar and stir until it has dissolved. Cook for 15 minutes until the fatty oils begin to separate.

5 Add the fresh coriander and mint, cook for 3 minutes then carefully remove using a ladle and sieve. Discard the used herbs.

6 Fill a second pan with boiling water and place over a medium heat. Add the noodles and cook for 5 minutes, strain once done.

7 While you wait for the noodles, add the prawns to the soup and cook for 2 minutes.

8 Portion the noodles into serving bowls, then cover with soup and any optional toppings to your taste.

Chef's tips

If shrimp paste cannot be found, replace with 2 extra tablespoons of fish sauce. Enhance the flavour and presentation further by topping with extra coriander, mint, fresh chilli and cashew nuts.

Laksa

Josh Garcia is an independent, autistic artist who paints traditional and digital art including vintage arts in 1930's style, 80's cartoons, 90's anime and fanart. He recently held his first ever solo exhibition 'Retroverse' in ArtWorks' virtual gallery.

For this mixed media piece he used watercolour paint, watercolour crayons and regular crayons. Josh was inspired by St Patrick's Day plus the myths and folklore of Irish culture. By creating this artwork he also learned about historical themes and Celtic symbols, which he would like to incorporate again in future work.

Ireland

Artist: Josh Garcia
Commissioned by: ArtWorks South Yorkshire

Colcannon

1kg potatoes, chopped, peeled if you prefer

150g butter

2 spring onions, sliced

1 stalk of rosemary

5 handfuls of kale

125ml double cream

1 bacon rasher, sliced

Salt and pepper to taste

Colcannon

60 Mins

Serves **4**

One of Ireland's best known dishes, Colcannon is an excellent addition to a Sunday roast.

Method

1   Place a large pan over a medium heat and boil the potatoes with a few pinches of salt for 20 minutes or until soft.

2   While you wait for the potatoes, place a small pan over a low heat and add 50g of butter, the double cream and rosemary. Cook gently for 7 minutes stirring continuously to prevent burning or a skin forming. Taste the cream to check that the flavour of the rosemary is noticeable then remove from the heat.

3   Strain the potatoes then mash in a large bowl before slowly pouring in the cream, using a sieve to catch and discard the rosemary. Add additional salt to taste until the mash is to your liking.

4   Place a frying pan over a medium heat and add 50g of butter. Add the bacon slices and fry until crispy then leave to one side.

5   Use the same pan to fry your spring onions and kale. Cook until the kale has wilted.

6   Mix the kale and spring onions into the mashed potatoes. Place in a large serving bowl then top with bacon and the remaining piece of butter.

Chef's tips

Add a little milk to the mash for a softer texture. Omit the bacon for a vegetarian version.

6 sausages

300g smoked bacon, chopped

800g potatoes, peeled and chopped

2 brown onions, sliced

2 carrots, chopped into large pieces

3 leeks, sliced

1 stick of celery, chopped

500ml chicken stock

4 large rosemary sprigs

4 large thyme sprigs

Handful of fresh parsley, chopped

3 garlic cloves, partially crushed with the side of a knife

2 tbsps vegetable oil

Salt and pepper to taste

Coddle

 120 Mins

 Serves 4

A potato and pork one-pot which works any night of the week.

Method

1 Pre-heat the oven to 180°C. Use a small piece of string to tie together your rosemary and thyme sprigs into a tight bundle then leave to one side.

2 Place a high sided oven-safe pan with lid, or Dutch oven, over a medium heat and add 1 tablespoon of vegetable oil. Fry the sausages until browned on all sides, then remove to a side plate.

3 Next fry the bacon until crispy, then remove to a side plate.

4 Add the carrots and fry until browned and caramelised then remove to a side plate. At this point your pan may have a brown oily residue from all the frying. If so, remove the pan from the heat and allow to cool before carefully wiping clean with kitchen roll.

5 Return the pan to a medium heat and add a further tablespoon of vegetable oil. Once hot, add the onions, celery and the herb bundle together with a pinch of salt. Cook for 10 minutes or until the onions have softened, stirring throughout.

6 Add the leeks, garlic cloves, carrots and a splash of water. Combine and cook with the lid on for 5 minutes.

7 Once the leeks have softened, add the potatoes and mix together. Add the sausages, bacon, stock and parsley.

8 Cover with the lid and cook for 1 hour and 45 minutes in the oven or until the potatoes are soft.

Chef's tips

In this recipe we have added the garlic, rosemary and thyme for extra background flavour. To make a vegan version omit the bacon, use plant-based sausages and switch to vegetable stock.

Coddle

Hannah Rich is an award-winning creative and illustration artist. Based in the coastal city of Sunderland, she graduated in 2017 with a First Class B.A. in Illustration and Design. She has since attracted clients from across the UK, USA and Ireland. Hannah's first solo exhibition took place at the Hilton Hotel Newcastle Gateshead in 2018. Her art now belongs in collections at Congress House in London, Rodeo Drive in Beverly Hills, California, and in other big American cities such as Houston, San Francisco and Baltimore. Tyra Banks, Seth Rogen, B.J. Novak and Vanessa Hudgens have all also supported Hannah's illustrations online.

This piece depicts a traditional Malaysian mask and uses illustrations drawn by families supported by More Than Grandparents, a charity which is part of the Sunderland Family Arts Network and is run by and for kinship carers and their families.

Malaysia

Title: Mask of Malaysia
Artist: Hannah Rich
Website: www.hannahrich.net
Illustrations: Lily (7), Oliver (11), Poppie (5), Katherine (9), Xzander (7), Hayley (5), Alison (9), Katie (9), Bobbie (5), Tia (9), Natalia (4), Ava (7) and Imme (18 months)
Commissioned by: Sunderland Family Arts Network

Nasi Goreng

Nasi Goreng

 40 Mins   Serves **4**

A great way to use up rice from the previous evening, Nasi Goreng is perfect for cutting down on waste.

For the sauce

9 tbsps fish sauce

6 tbsps kecap manis

3 tbsps chilli sauce

3 tbsps tomato purée

1 tbsp vinegar

1 garlic clove, crushed

1 red chilli, finely chopped

1 thumb-sized piece of ginger, peeled and grated

For the rice

350g rice, pre-cooked and left until cold

1 shallot, sliced

2 garlic cloves, crushed

1 red chilli, finely chopped

1 thumb-sized piece of ginger, peeled and grated

1 lemongrass stalk, diced

1 tsp ground nutmeg

80g cherry tomatoes

80g green beans, ends removed and cut into thirds

4 eggs, 1 per person

Optional toppings

½ cucumber, sliced

3 spring onions, sliced

Handful of fresh tomatoes, chopped

Method

1 Combine all the sauce ingredients in a mixing bowl and leave to one side.

2 Place a large pan or wok over a medium heat and add the vegetable oil. Once hot add the green beans, cook for 5 minutes then add the tomatoes and shallots, frying for a further 5 minutes. Stir throughout.

3 Next add the garlic, ginger, chilli, lemongrass and nutmeg. Cook for 2 minutes and reduce to a low heat if necessary to prevent burning.

4 Return to a medium heat and add the pre-cooked rice. Break up any clumps as you stir through.

5 Once the rice is hot, add the sauce and cook for 5 minutes stirring occasionally.

6 While you wait, place a non-stick frying pan over a medium heat on a separate hob and add a dash of vegetable oil. Fry 1 egg per person.

7 Portion up the rice on separate plates. Cover with a fried egg and garnishes of your choosing.

Chef's tips

A beaten egg or two is often used to add extra protein. To do this, add the egg at the start before frying the green beans. Allow the egg to set for a moment then break it up with a spatula into bits. Traditionally, shrimp paste is used but we have substituted it with fish sauce as this is easier to source.

250g basmati or jasmine rice, washed

300ml water

50g dried shrimps

200g white fish

50g desiccated coconut

2 stalks of lemongrass, finely chopped

15 Makrut lime leaves, finely chopped

3 shallots, thinly sliced

Handful of fresh mint, finely chopped

Handful of fresh coriander, finely chopped

Handful of fresh basil, finely chopped

4 tbsps fish sauce

Juice of 3 limes

1 tbsp vegetable oil

Salt to taste

Nasi Ulam

105
Mins

Serves
4

This rice, herb and fish dish takes time to prepare but rewards with a unique flavour.

Method

1 Rehydrate the dried shrimps by placing them in a bowl with a touch of boiling water. Strain the water then mash the shrimps in a pestle and mortar.

2 Place the shrimps in a small pan over a medium heat and toast until dry and dark orange. Remove from the heat and leave to cool.

3 Repeat the process of rehydration for the desiccated coconut and then toast. The coconut will take approx. 10 minutes to fully dry out, stir constantly to prevent sticking. Once done, grind down with the pestle and mortar then leave to one side.

4 Place the rice in a pan with 300ml of water. Bring to the boil then place a lid on the pan. Reduce to the lowest heat that maintains a simmer and cook for approx. 10 minutes.

5 Add the vegetable oil to a large frying pan over a medium heat. Fry the fish for 5 minutes or until cooked through. Place to one side and break up.

6 Once the rice has cooked, combine all the ingredients together in a bowl and mix thoroughly.

Chef's tips

Take time to chop the herbs finely as this will help the flavours to better integrate. Dried shrimp is traditionally used however these aren't always easy to find, so small fresh prawns are a good alternative. Several ingredients such as torch ginger flower, kerisik and pepper leaves have been omitted or replaced as they can be difficult to source however they can sometimes be found in specialist food shops.

Nasi Ulam

Creating artwork that truly represents the multi-cultural, multi-faceted nature of the USA was a huge task. However it was perfect for Inspire Arts, long-time collaborators and studio holders at The Art House.

The piece stemmed from initial conversations with artist, Inspire group leader and workshop facilitator Jo Cottam. Inspired by the recipes, Jo wanted the group to produce an image that combined the rich heritage of the deep South, synonymous with Jambalaya, and the playful Americana innocence that a milkshake brings to mind.

To kick off the project with the group, 2 photographs representing the idea behind the work (a New Orleans street during Mardi Gras and a classic roadside diner encrusted with bubble-gum pink and blue neon) were converted into black and white line drawings. Over the course of a number of sessions, group members were encouraged to use any creative medium to make interpretations of the line drawings, incorporating their own personal thoughts, feelings and memories of the USA into the work.

Finally, the group's individual pieces were scanned and digitally manipulated to create a collage. The effect of combining each person's work, featuring various techniques and mediums into a final abstract piece, is the best representation of the melting pot that is the USA they could imagine.

Artists: Robert, Rosemary, Lesley and Emma
Group Leaders: Jo Cottam, Diana Ellis and Antje Rayner
Graphic Designer: Chloe Wybrant
Commissioned by: The Art House

Jambalaya

300g basmati rice, washed

500ml chicken stock

100g prawns

300g smoked, normal or chorizo sausages, cut into chunks

300g chicken breast, cut into chunks

1 brown onion, diced

1 green bell pepper, cut into chunks, core and seeds removed

2 sticks of celery, sliced

1 courgette, chopped

4 garlic cloves, crushed

400g tin of plum tomatoes

5 tbsps Cajun seasoning

2 tsps thyme leaves

2 tsps oregano

3 tbsps vegetable oil

Tabasco to taste

Salt and pepper to taste

Jambalaya

120 Mins

Serves 4-6

This rice based one pot is a staple of Cajun cooking.

Method

1   Place a large pan over a medium heat and add the vegetable oil. Add the sausages and fry for 5 minutes, then remove to a side plate.

2   Add the onions, celery and pepper to the pan, fry until soft. Add the garlic and cook for 2 minutes, stirring frequently to ensure it doesn't burn.

3   Next add the courgette and cook for a further 5 minutes or until soft.

4   Add the Cajun seasoning and oregano. Combine and cook for 5 minutes, stirring constantly to ensure the spices don't burn.

5   Next add the tinned plum tomatoes, thyme and tabasco. Stir and break up any large pieces of tomato.

6   Add the cooked sausages and the chicken. Cook for 5 minutes or until the outer sides of the chicken have whitened.

7   Add the chicken stock and rice. Bring to the boil then place a lid on the pan. Reduce to a low heat and cook for approx. 10-15 minutes.

8   Add the prawns, ensuring they are submerged. Cook for a further 5 minutes or until pink, depending on the size/variety you are using.

9   Check that the chicken and rice have cooked through, then serve.

Chef's tips

Garnish with coriander and spring onions if you would like a little extra freshness. You can make the dish vegan friendly by replacing the meat and seafood elements with oven roasted vegetables such as sweet potato, red onion, carrots, courgette or squash. Just add them in with the rice at the end and mix together. Don't forget to switch your stock to a vegan friendly alternative too.

1 banana, chopped

500g strawberries, stalks removed

200ml milk

2 tbsps clear honey

Handful of fresh mint leaves, finely chopped (optional)

Strawberry & Banana Milkshake

10 Mins **Serves 2** **Veg**

A healthy, fresh take on a classic.

Method

1 Place all the ingredients in a blender and blitz!

Chef's tips

Try adding other fruit such as blueberries. Use plant-based milk and honey substitutes to make it vegan friendly.

Accessible Arts & Media's artwork was inspired by the colours, music, food and people of Libya. Due to the Covid-19 pandemic they were still delivering sessions remotely. So, the challenge was to come up with a simple, effective and accessible way for participants to create their artwork at home.

They worked with Adam Higton, a York-based artist, to create simple black and white templates based on their research about Libya. Templates were sent to participants prior to their online sessions, along with packs of coloured tissue paper.

The templates represent a Libyan oud, flute, drum, pomegranate, coffee, people and the star found on the national flag. Participants worked with Adam in online sessions to fill their templates with colour, taking inspiration from the images found and the music listened to during the session. Their aim was to express the vibrancy of Libyan culture through colour.

Adam took everyone's collages and digitised them, overlaying the colours from the different pieces of tissue paper. They are a reminder of the Libyan pottery, mosaics and glass looked at as part of their research. Some of the digitised pieces were selected and brought together in the final artwork. The participants had lots of fun being creative together in their sessions and they hope this artwork makes you smile as much as it does them!

Artist: Adam Higton
Commissioned by: Accessible Arts & Media

Kaak Malih

1 ½ tbsps sesame seeds

150g plain flour

1 ½ tsps baking powder

1 ½ tsps salt

80ml milk

80g unsalted butter

1 egg, beaten

1 tbsp olive oil

Kaak Malih

120 Mins **Serves 8** **Veg**

These savoury biscuits are great with a coffee.

Method

1   Sieve the plain flour into a large mixing bowl together with the baking powder and 1 tsp of salt.

2   Dry fry the sesame seeds on a medium heat for 2 minutes or until a light browning appears. Remove from the heat and leave to cool.

3   Melt the butter in a large pan over a medium heat.

4   Once melted, pour the butter into a separate mixing bowl and combine with the milk and olive oil. Begin to add this liquid to the bowl of flour, a little at a time, mixing with a fork at first then kneading by hand. You're aiming for a soft, elastic ball of dough.

5   Wrap the dough in cling film and leave in the fridge for 1 hour.

6   Pre-heat the oven to 180°C.

7   Remove the dough from the fridge and divide it into 2 equally sized pieces. Roll each into thin sausage shapes approx. 1 cm thick.

8   Cut the sausage shapes to approx. 10 cm in length and bend into a U shape. Plait the 2 long parts of the U into a rope-like shape. Coat the plaits with beaten egg then top with the toasted sesame seeds.

9   Prepare a baking tray with greaseproof paper, then place the plaits on top and cook in the oven for 15 minutes or until golden brown.

Chef's tips

If you are unsure about the folding technique, practise beforehand with a rolled out bit of sticky tack and try to replicate the plait shape.

600g lamb meat, diced

150g orzo

2 brown onions, diced

200g fresh tomatoes, chopped

3 tbsps tomato purée

4 garlic cloves, crushed

1 litre chicken stock

120g chickpeas, drained and rinsed

Handful of fresh parsley, chopped

4 tbsps dried mint

1 ½ tsps cayenne pepper

½ tsp ground turmeric

1 tsp ground cinnamon

1 cinnamon stick

1 tsp paprika

½ tsp ground coriander

½ tsp ground cumin

Juice of half a lemon

2 tbsps olive oil

Salt and pepper to taste

Shorba

180 Mins

Serves 4-6

A totally unique stew that combines pasta, lamb, tomato and mint.

Method

1 Place a large pan over a medium heat and add the olive oil. Add the lamb meat and begin to fry. Season with salt and cook until caramelisation begins to appear on the pieces of lamb. Straining and saving the juices in a bowl may help with this. Once done, remove all meat and juices to a side dish.

2 Next add a dash more olive oil to the pan and begin frying the onions and cinnamon stick. Cook for 10 minutes or until the onions are soft.

3 Add the garlic, fresh tomatoes and tomato purée. Cook for a further 5 minutes and burst the tomatoes as they soften.

4 Reduce to a low heat then add the cayenne pepper, turmeric, paprika, ground cinnamon, ground coriander and ground cumin. Combine and cook for 10 minutes, stirring frequently to ensure the spices don't burn. Add a dash of water if necessary to loosen from the pan.

5 Add the parsley, stock, lamb meat and any excess juices. Raise the heat to a simmer and cook for 1 hour 45 minutes or until the meat is tender.

6 Next add the orzo and cook for 7 minutes.

7 Add the dried mint and a squeeze of lemon juice. Cook for a final 2 minutes then serve.

Chef's tips

Don't hold back on the dried mint as it gives this dish its real identity. Take your time cooking the lamb, be patient and wait for it to soften.

Shorba

3 litres water

1 chicken carcass

2 celery sticks, roughly chopped

2 carrots, roughly chopped

2 brown onions, halved with skin on

3 garlic cloves, halved

Handful of fresh rosemary

Handful of fresh thyme

½ tbsp of black peppercorns, whole

Chicken Stock

180 Mins

Serves 3-4

This versatile stock can be used as the base for a variety of soups and is full of flavour!

Method

1   Add the oil to a large pan over a medium heat. Fry the onions, carrots and celery sticks until they are slightly browned.

2   Add the water and chicken carcass, bones and all. Bring to the boil, reduce to a medium heat and add all the other ingredients.

3   Cover with a lid and leave to reduce for 2½ hours.

4   Using a sieve, separate the liquid from the other ingredients. Discard the chicken remains and vegetables as they will be tasteless. Use your stock as required.

Chef's tips

Using a leftover chicken carcass from a roast is perfect but you could just as easily use a selection of bones from thighs, drumsticks or wings if you have those to hand instead.

Vegetable Stock

180 Mins　　**Serves 3-4**　　**Vegan**

This traditional vegetable stock is perfect for soup and gravy!

3 litres water

3 celery sticks, roughly chopped

2 carrots, roughly chopped

2 brown onions, halved with skin on

4 garlic cloves, halved

Handful of fresh rosemary

Handful of fresh thyme

1 tbsp of black peppercorns, whole

Method

1   Add the oil to a large pan over a medium heat. Fry the onions, carrots and celery sticks until they are slightly browned.

2   Add the water and bring to the boil. Reduce to a medium heat and add all the other ingredients.

3   Cover with a lid and leave to reduce for 2½ hours.

4   Using a sieve, separate the liquid from the other ingredients. Discard the vegetable remains as they will be tasteless. Use your stock as required.

Chef's tips

Leave the skins on the onions for extra colour. Add extra herbs to create your own signature stock.

Order copies of the *Secret Dishes From Around the World* series at: www.bouncebackfood.co.uk/shop

The original Secret Dishes From Around the World (2019) is packed full of vegetarian and vegan recipes and beautifully illustrated by Libby Element.

Secret Dishes From Around the World 2 (2020) contains recipes from 20 countries and original designs by 20 artists based in Greater Manchester, Cheshire & North Wales.

Once again, thank you for supporting the development of our community cookery school by buying this book. We hope you enjoyed the artwork, recipes and food photography!

As the economic impact of Covid-19 starts to unfold, it is clear that we need to speed up the development of our community cookery school so that we are able to support more extensively people living in food poverty nationwide. Our team in central Manchester is focused on building delivery teams in towns and cities across the UK that are able to support people living in food poverty by:

- Ensuring their nearest foodbank is stocked with good quality items of nutritious food.

- Providing them the opportunity to learn how to cook for free and supporting them with career progression in the food industry.

- Enabling them to learn about cooking, budgeting, nutrition, meal planning and reducing food waste through the provision of free access to our Cooking & Nutrition Portal.

- Providing free hot nutritious meals at community events.

There are a number of ways to further support our mission to fight food poverty nationwide. You could:

- Recommend this book and the *Secret Dishes From Around the World* series to friends and family if they're looking for a gift that gives twice.

- Become a member of our community cookery school! There are 3 tiers available, all providing you with 12 months access to our online Cooking & Nutrition Portal. Sign up today: www.bouncebackfood.co.uk/membership

- Take part in one of our online cookalongs and learn how to cook 2 exciting recipes from a 'secret' country. Thanks to our **buy one, give one** model, your ticket helps us allocate free places to our partner charities. You could also purchase one of our gift vouchers as a present for a foodie.

- Fund the provision of hot, nutritious meals for people struggling to access food via our Community Meal Drives. Pledge directly at www.bouncebackfood.co.uk/shop

- Listen to our podcast 'Share Your Secrets' which celebrates the diversity of food, art and community. Episodes include interviews with the artists involved in the production of *Secret Dishes From Around the World 2* plus insights about community and culture from people in the featured countries. You can listen for free on a variety of platforms including: Apple Podcasts, Spotify and YouTube.

With your help, we will be able to accelerate the development of our community cookery school as we scale up our fight against food poverty across the UK. Thank you!

Much love,

The Bounceback Team

Index